Advance Praise

King of Doubt is a testament to the power of memoir to illuminate the past, redeem its shadows, and find wisdom and strength in life's mysteries. Beautifully written, suspenseful, and brave, Peter Gibb's saga of self-discovery will brace you with its honesty and enrich you with its heart. Buy this book!

—Mark Matousek, author of
The Boy He Left Behind

King of Doubt is a story of adventuresome times, of intimate relationships, of inner determination. I was drawn in emotionally, riveted to every chapter. This book is beautifully written, a work of art, about growing up male, about taking on the world, about loving and not giving up on life. A tour de force!

—Susan Krieger, Stanford University, author of
*Come, Let Me Guide You: A Life Shared with a
Guide Dog* and *Things No Longer There: A Memoir
of Losing Sight and
Finding Vision*

A memoir of confession and triumph, *King of Doubt* deserves every reader's attention. The story sweeps forward with compelling intensity, in language that is detailed, humorous, and graceful. Here is a man who's taken the road less traveled and savored it fully.

—Kent Nelson, author of *The Spirit Bird*, winner
of the Drue Heinz prize for literature

King of Doubt by Peter Gibb sends you across continents and time in an unforgettable journey of self-discovery. With the soul of a poet and the rich language of an artist, Gibb illuminates everyday life and, in the process, our own lives. Here is a memoir to savor.

—Gayle Lynds, *New York Times* best-selling
author of *The Assassins* and *The Book of Spies*

Courageously written, an inspiring tribute to the human spirit. Highly recommended.

—Brad Knickerbocker,
The Christian Science Monitor

With stunning prose, *King of Doubt* will take readers on an enthralling journey across time, continents, and the various roller coasters that make up life. This memoir serves as a tribute to human courage, while it examines the tiny beautiful mysteries that touch everyone.

—Belo Cipriani, *The Bay Area Reporter*,
author of *Blind*

In this unusually compelling and inspiring memoir, Gibb draws from a rich tapestry of personal experiences, describing a life that many seemingly successful people lead these days: victories that feel transitory or undeserved, defeats that bite deeper and linger longer, and an underlying pervasive self-doubt. Yet the author's commendable honesty in facing facts eventually brings him to embrace the admirable person that had lain within.

—William Ruddiman, Climate Scientist, author of
Plows, Plagues and Petroleum

King of Doubt is riveting, emotionally honest, and brilliantly written. What at first seems like a charming coming-of-age tale transforms into a sharing of personal anguish. Told with sophisticated, self-deprecating humor, the story spins toward tragedy before being pulled back by unexpected events. For those who enjoy masterful writing and great storytelling, I highly recommend Peter Gibb's *King of Doubt*.

—Marilee Zdanek, author of *The Right-Brain Experience, Inventing the Future, Splinters in My Pride, Someone Special*

The test of a good memoir is to be engaged in the story, someone else's story, and at the same time to be drawn into reviewing one's own life more deeply. *King of Doubt* succeeds on both counts. From the pain of childhood in a foreign country, to the hopelessness of deep depression, to the uplifting victory of discovering deeper meaning in life, Peter Gibb lays it out for us. We experience our own struggles and successes as we read of Peter's.

—Leon Pyle, PhD, Psychoanalytic Psychotherapist

King of Doubt

Peter Gibb

Published by Wheatmark®
2030 East Speedway Boulevard, Suite 106
Tucson, Arizona 85719
www.wheatmark.com

ISBN: 978-1-62787-445-8 (paperback)
ISBN: 978-1-62787-446-5 (ebook)
LCCN: 2016950182

"Not all who wander are lost."—J.R.R.Tolkein

"No, but most of them are."—Anonymous

For Wendy
My love—no doubt about that.

I have occasionally adjusted timing and consolidated events for brevity. I have changed some names to protect privacy and altered minor details for the sake of dramatic intensity. It's a story, my truth, throughout, a mostly true memoir.

Acknowledgments

It takes one finger to strike a letter on the keyboard, but a team to produce a book. I was fortunate to have a great team beside me.

My number-one cheerleader was my wife, Wendy, who waved the flag, asked the tough questions, and supported me with love and understanding throughout. She not only lived through much of this story at my side, she then had to relive it through the writing of the book. She survived to tell the story, and—thanks to her—so did I.

Every writer needs a coach and editor. I had the best, Sarah Lovett (http://sarahlovett.com/). She kept me true to the task, gave me straight and useful feedback, and never let me feel alone in what can be very lonely work.

I feel deep appreciation for my beta readers; Bill Ruddiman and Steve Klingelhofer, friends from high school days, were still there for me, all these years later. Cynde Christie and Gay Knight appeared magically and were among the first to read a full draft and lend the kind of support that kept me going forward. Joy Drake Silver and Leon Pyle read later versions and held up the mirror that every writer needs.

The team at Wheatmark were wonderful and patient

with a writer heading into the marketing fray for the first time. Grael Norton, Mindy Burnett, and Lori Conser were knowledgeable, patient, and supportive throughout.

Finally, I would like to thank my parents, Charles and Mary Louise Gibb, neither of whom lived to read a word of this book, but who nevertheless breathed life into every page. I hope I have not been too harsh on them. I hold them in deep love and gratitude for all they did for me.

I consider myself lucky and blessed to have lived the life I have and to have had the chance to write a book about the journey.

Chapter 1

"Are ya ready, lads?" When the master's voice boomed, even the rain paused to listen.

Twenty-three lads squirmed, waiting for the start of the race. Toes twitched and eyes searched. Wee ones were these boys, but fierce as the weather that slammed in from the Atlantic, thrashing the west coast of Scotland.

My lips quivered. I needed to pee.

Twenty-three lads scratched their private parts. Parents stomped their soaked galoshes and fidgeted with the buttons on their slickers.

"On yer marks." The master's voice again. The boys squeezed tight their bottoms.

Twenty-three pair of shoes pawed the mud, racehorses chomping at the starting gate, muscles taut. My shoelace was untied. My shorts hung low. I was no racehorse. Made in the USA, from different stock than the Scots, I was the only Yank, and a scrawny one at that.

"Get set."

Twenty-three hearts thumped eagerly. One heart trembled.

"Go!"

Off they went. Toes and feet and legs and arms, small

King of Doubt   1

but mighty, intrepid soldiers of fortune, sloshing through the mud of win or die. Twenty-three muddied bodies. One burning heart, anxious...but not about winning. "Will they like me?" was the fire that stoked that one, smoldering heart.

We were at Campusdoon School for boys in Ayr, Scotland, my first school, my first field day. I hoped there would never be another. Campusdoon rose out of the mist, so close to the ocean I smelled the brine from the sea each morning as my mother drove me up the winding driveway to the old stone castle that was now Campusdoon School.

On the field, the lads sped forward, while my spindly legs quivered like stalks of beach grass in the wind. All eyes followed Harold Tweedy. Harold was the fastest boy in Scotland, the only boy with a white zagged stripe on his blue shorts. Harold sped to the front of the pack as expected, while I stumbled about, dazed, chewing my thumbnail, half forgetting the race, searching the crowd and my classmates for a sign, any sign, of approval. *Am I okay? Am I doing it right? Do you like me now?*

Someone yelled, "Go, Harold. Go, laddie." Harold was halfway to the finish while I staggered about, lost amid the also-rans.

The pack surged forward. And then, suddenly, a gasp from the crowd. "What is it? What's happened?" "It's Harold. He's..." Harold slipped. He righted himself. He slipped again. Now he was down in the mud, and behind him, McDougal tripped over Harold and then Buchanan and Burns, and following them, MacDonald and McBride and Calhoun, falling all over one another, tripping in the mud, screeching like cracked bagpipes, trying to get up, tripping sideways and backward, slipping and sprawling and stumbling, and then Bruce and MacGregor glanced over their shoulders to see, and down they went too. Boys in the mud and groans in the crowd.

A father's voice sounded the national alarm. "Blimey, would ya look at that little bugger on the end. The wee one. The Yank, isn't it? He's the only one still standing. He's goin' ta win the bloody race."

Heads swiveled. Eyes bored through me. I floundered, blowing about like a leaf in the wind, but somehow moving forward. My mother's voice, a siren from the crowd, sang out: "Go, Peter. Run." I lurched, one foot in front of the other—uncertain who? what? why?—and then, I stumbled across a white line and stood, shaking, surrounded by gray flannel pants and big umbrellas and the bug-eyed master, his hand gripping my shoulder, too tight.

The master steered me to a long table, covered by a muddy once-upon-a-time-white tablecloth and the prizes, boxed and lined up like the houses along Wheatfield Road. Dazed as a daisy in winter, I grabbed the table for support, wiped my snotty nose, and squished the warm mud in my hands. I turned, horrified, at the jumble of my classmates, a few now staggering toward the finish, others still struggling to right themselves in the mud. *Why am I here, alone with the prizes?* And the question that glowed neon in every cell of my body, *Will the lads like me now? Am I okay?* The glob of goo in my stomach told me that I had won the race, but lost something...something, what? Hard to say. Something more important than a race on a muddy field.

The master's face was drawn and glum. He patted my head. We posed for a photo. He slipped me the prize.

"Well, laddie, here ya go. Jus' like a sneaky Yank, found a dry patch o' ground over yonder, ya did."

Parents shook their heads and slunk off into the mist. "I dinna ken. A dark day fer Sco'land it is, this scraggly Yank snatchin' tha' winner's prize from our lads."

Calhoun sneered and tossed a well-formed mud cake at me. "Here 'tis, lad, have some good Sco'ish mud now, will ya, so ya ken wha' tha' rest o' us ran through."

Calhoun's mud cake struck my heart.

The prize was a box of toy soldiers. I held them tight to my chest as if these ten tin figures could rescue me from shame. I didn't deserve the prize. I stared at the carnage on the field. "No!" I screamed, and the rain swallowed my wail.

*

We sat around the kitchen table, at dinner, the night of the race. Dad smiled and clapped his hands. "What a lad! You bloody well showed 'em." I loved my dad. Of course, I never told him. Words like "love" were shoved to the back shelf of the junk closet in our house, wedged between old magazines and broken pencils.

"What a thrilling race!" Mom said. "A proud day for America."

"Mother Margaretha told us we'll have a cooking class at school," my sister Virginia said. "There'll be a prize for the best cake."

"They don't give prizes for cooking," I said.

"They do too." Virginia was two years older than me and a know-it-all.

"I haven't seen your prize soldiers," Mom said. "Have you played with them yet?" Mom was American, differ-ert. Her permed curls bound magically together despite the Scottish gales. She held her skirt tight around her knees when we walked to the beach. "The weather at that race was shocking," she said. "I'm sure it's sunny and warm in Washington. I was not brought up for Scottish weather."

*

Dad had recently moved us from Washington, DC, to the west coast of Scotland. A retired British Navy pilot, he had opened a pilots' training school in Ayr. Mom was unsure if Ayr was the right place to bring up her children. "What's so great about a kilt?" she asked when I wanted to wear my kilt to bed. "In America, all the boys wear pants."

It was 1947. The war had been over two years, but rationing was still part of life in Scotland. Three eggs per week for a family of four, one quart of milk. Every day, Mom tore out two small green tickets from our ration book. "A crying shame, what we put up with here," she said.

I was learning my way around Ayr—where to hear the bagpipes, which of the Scottish lads were most likely to torment me, and where Mom hid the cookies. I both loved and feared Scotland, where the wind blew stronger and the rain fell harder than any other spot on earth. Head down, slicker up, feet swimming in galoshes, two sizes too big, I battled the wind and my classmates daily. *I won the race, they have to like me now. Don't they?* I was getting used to the burr—lads who sounded like they were talking with a mouth full of pebbles. The school uniform was scratchy— blue gabardine shirts and a maroon and blue striped tie, knee-high gray socks and gray wool shorts. My knees turned blue as the sea every morning. On warm days, they thawed out by three.

Behind our house, the backyard was wild, rocky, and defiant, like Scotland. Before the race, I'd practiced there, racing Harold Tweedy around the yard, but he hopped faster than I ran. Harold was a winner. I was a loser. I hid my prize soldiers under the bed. The masters and the boys, the whole school would soon realize their mistake and come knocking at my front door, pointing fingers and jeering, demanding that I return the prize.

Except that Dad found and opened the box of soldiers first. "Lookee here!" he exclaimed. "Aren't they wonderful? They'll remind you of the race. You must be so proud."

Looking at the soldiers gave me nightmares. I dreamed the boys from Campusdoon were coming after me, their eyes on fire, their bayonets fixed, like the soldiers, ready to gore me. At dinner the next night, I couldn't eat. Mom gave me an extra helping of pudding. "For the fastest boy in Form One," she said.

I shoved my pudding away.

"Peter, what's the matter?"

I ran from the table. *They're coming. Coming to take the soldiers away. Coming to take me away. Winning the race didn't make them like me. It made them hate me more. I am a fake. The masters know it. The lads know it. Everyone knows it now.*

*

I continued to fool a few, mostly adults. I learned to say "Please" and "Thank you" and "May I be excused," not much else. My parents approved of me. My teachers approved of me. I approved of their approvals, never imagining that I was looping a noose around my neck that would continue to strangle me for four decades.

I made up a story that explained it all. I won a race. My parents applauded, assuming that coming in first meant I was a winner. But can you claim victory if you win a race and lose your soul? I was a loser. I was unworthy, a fake, maybe even a cheat. Year after year, I refined my story, packing in additional evidence of my nobodyness.

The first time you tell yourself a story about yourself, it's just that—a story. The second time you tell the same story, it becomes a theory. By the third time, it has morphed into The Truth, incontrovertible, self-evident, and eternal. I told myself my loser story, first thing in the morning and last thing at night, on the playground and at dinner, over and over, day after day, year after year, until it became me. I became the story. I became the fraud. At first, the voice of the fraud was just one of many voices inside my brain, but it was the loudest and the most persistent. It drowned out all others. I didn't realize that the fraud story I told myself was one of a thousand thoughts. I didn't realize that the fraud story—like all thoughts—was real, but not necessarily true. I didn't realize that I had signed a pact with the devil: I'd be a fraud, I'd cut away my heart, if that's what it took, to make others approve of me. The deal banished me from society, deep into the dungeons of doubt, where the lost souls of life roam in dark catacombs, reserved for the living and the damned.

*

Dad displayed my prize tin soldiers, spread out in a

row, on their very own shelf, on the bookcase, in the living room, across from the front door. "Beautiful. Proud. Ready for action. Just like you," Dad said. "Now everyone who comes to the house will see them, and I'll tell them the story of how you won the race."

The next day, when Mom and Dad were upstairs, I threw the soldiers into a bag. I fetched Dad's hammer from the chest in the front hallway, took the bag out to the front steps, and smashed the soldiers into a hundred pieces. I dug a hole in the garden and buried the pieces as deep as I could. Then I came back inside, returned the hammer to the chest in the front hallway, and sat down as if nothing had happened.

As soon as he came downstairs, Dad noticed. He shook his head. "Where is your prize? Where are the soldiers?"

I didn't answer. He dropped it, and Mom never asked.

As far as I know, the soldiers' remains are still buried deep in that hole, under the Scottish mud. We lived in Scotland for another year. We never talked about the soldiers—or the race—again.

Chapter 2

"You made it through high school, or you wouldn't be here, but now you're in the big leagues. Look to the one on your left. Look to the one on your right. One of you won't be here four years from now."

I am an entering freshman at Brown University, one of eight hundred brown beanies seated in an orientation session at Sayles Hall. The dean of students is trying—successfully in my case—to intimidate us. *Why is he looking right at me? Does he know I am a fraud? Does he know I have no right to be here?* I glance furtively at my classmate on the left, the one to my right. Both look confident, worldly, and intelligent. I look...well, let's just say I'd place my bets on them. My high school career swirls in my brain, how I had warmed the bench of life, waiting to get into the game. I'd wanted so desperately to be cool, but I was a loser. I worked at it; I'd tried hard and worried incessantly. The more I tried, the more I worried. The more I worried, the less cool I became.

College, I'm determined, is going to be different. It has to be. All I want is to be liked and accepted.

For a while, I think it's going to happen. I enter the freshmen tennis tournament. I win it. I run for Student

Union Board of Governors. I win. I rush two of the best fraternities. I am invited to join both. I have my eye on a girl. She smiles back. Life looks good, but the demons in my doubter's stomach are ravenous. There is no peace.

I make daily trips to the John Hay library. I research and document before I write anything, amass arguments and counter arguments, footnotes and bibliographies. Every word I write is built on my unconscious belief that if it is worth saying, someone has said it before, and if no one has said it, I will not dare to be the first. My professors nod politely. I'm not an embarrassment. My work is solid, competent. And boring.

*

On an ice-heavy day in early January, I slip into Psych 20, my first college psych class. I am eager finally to study the human spirit. I have no idea of the havoc that what I think of as my "Doubt" will eventually wreak in my life, but I am desperate to learn about these dark forces that invade my brain. This class is billed as a discussion format. I have a lot of questions.

Students file in from the cold, filling the room with clapping hands and stomping boots. In the background, an unmistakable high-pitched squeak. On one side of the room is a huge wall full of rats, cage after cage, filled by white rats with pink noses, long tails, and oversized ears, rat after rat, rat above rat and rat below rat. The rats are talking. The students are not.

We sit at tables in a circle. I survey the twenty or so other students. Enter a flagpole of a man in a gray suit that hangs off his shoulders like a rumpled sheet slung across a bed. He's wearing a navy blue beret, probably recycled from his great-grandfather's closet. A cigarette droops from his mouth. "I am Professor Temple," he scratches out in a dry voice. "All you need to know about psychology can be learned from a rat."

Professor Temple pads about in tiny, quiet shuffles across the room. He is half human and half...rat? I stare at him and I stare at the wall of rat cages. What have I gotten myself into?

"The rat is the star of this show," Professor Temple launches his opening lecture. "You will each have your own rat, which you will feed and clean and train in the ways and behaviors we will discuss. The rat will learn to do exactly what you condition it to do, nothing more and nothing less. In time, you will come to see how similar you are to your rat. If your rat dies due to your negligence, you fail the class. Any questions?"

No questions. I am assigned rat #599B-12. Professor Temple instructs us not to name our rats. I don't tell anyone, but secretly I name my rat "Iggy."

We study Pavlov's salivating dogs, Watson's experiment inducing fear into baby Albert, and Skinner's famous box, proving beyond doubt that all behavior is a conditioned response to reward and punishment. I condition Iggy. With nothing but pellets, I train him to press a bar and ring a bell. I learn about operant conditioning. I marvel how, with the right controls and conditioning, you can train a rat, just the way you can train a human. *Maybe Professor Temple is right. Maybe we are just like these rats. Do rats doubt themselves the way I do?*

A group of six of us—Wally, an imposing hulk from

New Jersey and the self-proclaimed leader of the group, nicknames us the "badass psychologists"—traipse regularly to the student union for coffee after class. Mostly I watch and listen while the group talks about rats and how to have fun at Professor Temple's expense. Our rats become little extensions of ourselves. I worry about Iggy. He doesn't seem to have friends.

"Professor Temple is right," Wally says. "We are rats. We are conditioned machines. Every decision I make is the result of years of operant conditioning, millions of tiny rewards and punishments since I was seconds old."

Bullshit, I sneer, but silently.

Wally is on a roll. "From the first moment when my mom smiled at me, I was being conditioned to behave in a certain way. I am my mother's conditioning. Nothing more, nothing less."

The badass psychologists nod their collective rat heads. I summon my one ounce of courage to speak up. "A conditioned rat can't make choices. He is controlled by his conditioning. I have free will. I can go out for coffee after class, or I can go back to my room. I can get up in the morning, or I can stay in bed. I make choices all the time. I am not my mother." Hearing my own words, I can't help thinking how much like my mother I am. How much like a rat I actually am. I don't talk about that. I want to appear cool.

Wally pours me a refill of coffee. "Thank you," I say.

"Why'd you say, 'Thank you'?" Wally leans in.

"It's…" For a fraction of a second I pause, maybe to think about why. In the silence, my heart begins to race. I rush to complete the sentence, the only, the obvious finish. "…polite."

Wally scoffs. "Years ago, your mother told you to say 'thank you' when someone gave you something." He tosses his head back. "You've internalized your mother. You are your mother's conditioning, the same as Iggy is your conditioning."

I clunk my coffee cup down in disgust. "No way. Free will—"

"—is an illusion," Wally cuts me off. "Your conditioning is so complete, you're oblivious to it."

I'm incensed. I want to discover who I am, to find my path so I can realize my potential. If I am nothing more than a conditioned rat, then I am even more a fraud than I'd imagined. "I'll prove it." Wally has a gleam in his eye now. "I've designed an experiment."

I miss what he says next, caught up inside my own head, arguing within myself. *I'm more than a conditioned rat. I want more than a sugar-coated rice crispy.* But when I try to pursue my soliloquy to the next level—*So who are you and what do you want?*—my mind hits a wall. *I don't know. I don't know who I am.* Eventually I tune back in to the conversation. Wally is describing his experiment. My eyes grow bigger. "You can't do that."

"Yes, I can," he says.

"It'll never work. If we're discovered, we'll get in trouble," I argue.

"Did your mother teach you to fear authority too?" Wally asks with a smirk. "This'll work. I'll give you two-to-one odds."

Wally lays out his three-phase, ingenious experiment. If it works—Wally, damn him, has never even heard the word "doubt"—then it proves Professor Temple's point, at

Professor Temple's expense. And if that's true, then why am I bothering with college, when my miserable existence is nothing more than a dramatized version of a rat in a cage, pressing a bar for more Rice Krispies.

Wally assigns individual students to record every stimulus and every response. He rubs his hands together in glee. The following Monday, as another snowstorm blankets the campus, we begin our experiment. I feel protective of Professor Temple and share my misgivings with Wally. "Next semester, we'll study you." He tosses his scarf around his neck. "You're a great rat."

Professor Temple lectures standing in front of the wall with the rat cages. Wally intends to change that. As soon as the professor approaches the rat wall, Wally's experiment kicks in, and the commotion starts. We rustle papers, drop books on the floor, stare out the window, and whisper to neighbors. Classic negative reinforcement. The moment Professor Temple moves, slinking over near the exit, we diligently attend his every word and gesture, take notes, ask questions, nod in appreciation for the wisdom we are absorbing. Temple smiles. Wally compiles the data. Professor Temple now teaches 86 percent of the time from an area not more than three feet from the exit door, far from his former perch next to the rat wall. Wally declares victory, treats us all to coffee, and explains Phase II. It is time to condition our professor to remove his beret, which he typically wears throughout the class, as soon as he enters the classroom. From the moment he passes through the door, until he removes his hat, we regress to our unruly behavior. Nothing the professor can do or say gets our attention. In frustration, he removes the beret for a moment. Instant transformation. All eyes on our beloved professor, pencils poised, twenty-five well-behaved, intellectually hungry, appreciative students. It works, perfectly. The beret is a thing of the past.

Phase III is the most ambitious. Temple is a heavy smoker. Wally explains the goal: "By the end of the semester, Professor Temple will have retired his Camels." Our tactics are the same as ever. After a month, he has cut down from an average of eight cigarettes per class to three. Hatless, pinned to the door, and minus his smokes, Professor Temple is gobbling down our Rice Krispies. Oblivious of his own conditioning, he lectures on about what rats can teach us.

I can't shake Wally's experiment from my mind. I fret over its meaning. Are Wally—and Professor Temple—right? Are we rats in a cage, conditioned automatons, acting out scripts that were programmed into us at an early age? What conditioning made me so dependent on outside approval? Am I a rat performing my mother's scripts? Can I get control over my own mind and body, or am I condemned to live on automatic forever?

If I am just a jumble of conditioned responses, then the "I" that I thought worthy of such attention and development is a fantasy. We are all pellet suckers, hungry rats performing for our supper.

"Now do you believe me?" Wally asks over coffee, once the experiment and the class are finished.

"Believe what?" I ask, knowing exactly what he's talking about.

"That you're a rat," he says with a triumphant grin.

*

Midway through my freshman year, I volunteer to work at Chapin House, a small psychiatric hospital in Providence. I want to get away from the rats. Mildred, a psychiatric nurse, is giving me a tour down a long, linoleum corridor, past an open door where a fiftyish woman calls out to me as we pass, "Hey, mister, you got some coffee? Bring me some coffee and I'll give you a blow job." Mildred closes the woman's door and moves on without comment.

Further down the hall, the door to room 413 is open. A mountain of a man sits on the bed, a small, shy curl of jet-black hair slipping down over his forehead, above his left eyebrow. He's wearing a muscleman T-shirt. He reminds me of Popeye the Sailor Man. Mildred keeps walking, but something draws me to this mountain. I stop in front of his door.

"Hi, I'm Peter."

He stares at the wall, rocking from side to side, his expression as blank as a field of fresh snow, but when he does finally look at me—a fraction of a second, then his eyes walk away again—I hear a call, a mournful, eerie wail. Is it real? Imagined? His? My own desperate scream? Quiet guys make me wonder what's going on inside. I move instinctively toward him.

"Leave him be," Mildred says.

"Why?"

"He's a sick man."

Is that lightning in his eyes I see when she says that, or is that my imagination too? "I want to talk to him."

"All the patients here have jobs to do," Mildred says, directing me away from room 413. "We simulate normal life as much as possible. They have to earn their privileges."

"What about him?" I nod toward the open door of room 413. "What does he do?"

"We have twenty-five patients on the ward at any one time." She pauses. "They told me you're a freshman at Brown, considering a career in mental health."

"How long has he been here?"

"Too long." Her brows step down. "Don't waste time with him. Besides, he's very strong, potentially dangerous. If you'll be coming this same time each week, you can sit in on group."

"What's his name?"

"Charlie, and he hasn't spoken a word to anyone in the nine months he's been here."

She drones on. When we finish the tour, I hang around and make conversation with other patients, but Charlie sits there in the middle of my mind, staring, huge and silent. I search for Mildred to ask her permission to visit him. No Mildred. My feet make the decision. I stand in front of 413, rap on the door. Nothing. "Charlie, can I come in?"

I enter the silence. The room is plain, a metal frame bed, one folding chair, no pictures, no sign of life, just the mountain of a man sitting on the bed surrounded by bone-white walls. I pull over the chair and sit near him. He looks straight ahead. Does he even realize I'm in the room? I look at his feet. I look at my feet. I look at the walls. Still white. So still, I can hear his heartbeat. Or is it mine? I take off my glasses, clean them with my sweater, put them back on. "There was a birthday party out there," I say. "You didn't go."

No response.

"They missed you."

As if the power has been turned off on his eyes.

"The nurse told me that everyone has a job. Do you have a job?" Feeble attempts at conversation. I'm talking to myself. I tell him that I'm a freshman from Washington, DC, a tennis player, planning on majoring in psychology. Don't know if he hears me or not.

Maybe it's the challenge. Certainly not the conversation, but when it's time to leave, I know I'm not done with Charlie. Maybe I identify with him. I've felt pretty alone and cut off for much of my life too. Growing up in England and Scotland, off to boarding school. Back and forth to the United States. Always struggling to please, to do it right, fighting the demons of doubt that roamed freely inside my brain. I never made friends easily.

Back on campus, I think about Charlie a lot. Why am I so drawn to him? In the beginning, I think of him as a "mental patient," myself as "normal." Different worlds. Then I realize how convenient and separating it is to put people in boxes. In high school, a common put-down was, "We'll send you to St. Elizabeth's (the local mental hospital)." The world was so easily divided into us and them. Does Charlie identify himself as a mental patient? Crazies and normals. Am I normal? I don't feel normal. *How would I be different if I were locked up? Would I still be me?*

When I return to Chapin, the first place I go is room 413. Charlie is there, just the way he was when I saw him the week before, hands under his hips, sitting on his bed, like he's waiting for something, but what?

One day I sit a little closer to him. "I'm lonely too," I tell him.

He looks at me. He looks inside me, in a way no one

ever has before. A wave pulses through me. Half fear, half excitement. Like something from another world. *I wonder... Where might we go with this?*

Before we can go anywhere, Mildred bursts in. "What are you doing here? I told you."

"Told me. What?" I inquire.

She looks at me, looks at Charlie, then steps between us. In a conspiratorial voice, "Dangerous. He... Come. Group is starting, down the hall. I want you to observe."

She ushers me out. I shamble down the hallway behind her, the squeak of her white, rubber-soled shoes like a nagging reprimand on an endless loop, "Naughty boy... naughty boy... naughty boy," and I'm five years old again and she is my mother and I follow along, two feet behind her.

Chapter 3

Our house in Scotland—"Three Gables"—named after the trio of yellow gables—peered out over the Atlantic like fishermen in slickers, crouching before the coming storm. We lived two hundred yards from the beach. From my upstairs bedroom window, I could see Ailsa Craig, the cone-shaped remains of an extinct volcano, rising from the ocean. Ailsa Craig was my muse, her mournful, mystical image like the song of the bagpipes, wailing in the fog. Ailsa Craig was the last remnant of a bygone era, her voice, the sound of sorrow. Did the Scots hear her melancholy? Or was I alone in this too?

Mom and Dad, Virginia, and I walked single file out to the beach for a picnic, fighting the wind, our feet obscured in the fog. Sand slapped at our eyes and our hair, burrowed into our ears and noses. Dad shielded the wicker picnic basket under his greatcoat. We settled behind a large rock, huddled together like lost sheep, and unwrapped our picnic. Our sandwiches were all sand, no wich.

"Listen," Dad cupped his ear. "Do you hear the piper on the glen?"

My legs sprang into action. "Can I go see, please?" We'd been in Scotland for six months, but I already loved the bagpipes. Their mournful wail summoned me and instantly I became a Scot, doomed, marching in one of the hundreds of hopeless campaigns these brave people fought against the English. Besides, anything was better than sitting on the beach, blasted by a wind that seemed about to toss me into the Atlantic.

"Go to the edge of the dunes. No farther. Come right back," Mom yelled as I headed out.

"Can I go too?" Virginia asked.

"Girls don't play bagpipes," I told her.

"And nor do little boys," Mom said, but I was gone, forgetting about the picnic, forgetting about Ailsa Craig and my family, up and over the dunes, snared by the piper's siren song, drawn to the bagpipe. The piper rose out of the fog and stood, on a mound on the glen, a god; he might have been there since the time of Robert the Bruce, dressed in full clan regalia: Hunting Stewart tartan kilt and sash across his mammoth chest, glengarry perched at a cocky angle on his head, tasseled sporran hanging from his waist, his deadly skean tucked into his white, knee-high socks. I was tiny as a grain of sand, and he was the roar of the ocean and the swell of the waves. I watched and listened as he played "Scotland the Brave." In that moment I knew the whole, proud, hopeless history of Scotland. All I wanted was to stand like this giant and play the pipes and be a Scot. *If I could do that, the lads would have to accept me.*

I crept as close as I dared. He must have sensed my awe. "Laddie, would you be wantin' to give 'er a go?"

"Can I touch it? Touch your bagpipe, please?"

"Touch it now, is that what ye' will?"

I nodded.

He knelt low, beside me. "Well, ye're a wee one. It's no the touchin' but ra'tha the playin'. Are ye' mindin' to try 'em?"

He took the strap from around his neck and looped it around mine, then shoved the bag under my elbow and the pipe in my mouth. "Now, blow, laddie, blow for all you're worth."

I blew. I huffed. I puffed. I blew until I was dizzy in the head. I thought I heard a tiny peep, but whether it was the wind's whistle or the bagpipe, I was unsure. When there was nothing left inside me, just before I was about to pass out, I passed the pipes back to the god without a word.

"Well, 'tis nay so easy as it ma' seem," he tucked the bag under his elbow, pumped the bag, and blared out another chorus of "Scotland the Brave." "Dinna ye' worry, lad. Soon, ye'll be playin' the pipes, I'm sure on it." I was less sure. I hunkered down against the wind and stumbled back to the beach, "Scotland the Brave" ever more distant in the background.

What is wrong with me? Why am I such a puny weakling? I imagined him telling his clan all about this feeble laddie— he must have realized I was not even a Scot—who tried, but couldn't make a sound.

"Did you find him?" Dad asked when I rejoined the family.

I nodded. "He let me blow his bagpipe."

"What did it sound like?" Virginia asked.

I looked back over the dunes, as if the sound might come marching over.

"You blew on his bagpipe!" Mom glowered. "Do you

have any idea of the germs swarming around his mouth piece?"

I shook my head. What were germs, and why were they so important? Mom marched us back home, the non-picnic over anyway. In the downstairs bathroom, she grabbed a bar of Yardley's soap. "Open your mouth." I tried to wriggle away, but she held my head tight and stuffed a soapy wash-cloth inside. "You can't be too careful," she frowned. "You have to learn these things."

The germs were gone. So was "Scotland the Brave."

✱

In May, Scotland burst into spring. On the playing fields of Campusdoon, where we had raced, the trees began to blossom. A huge chestnut tree, as old as King Arthur, ruled the grounds from a small knoll near the front gate. We boys scoured about for the biggest, hardest, toughest chestnuts to use for the game we called conquers. I found the perfect chestnut, round, well developed, dark and hard as a rock. I named him "Brownie." He lived in my pocket, where I could rub him for hours each day until he shone like a new penny.

I watched the lads and learned how to drill a hole and string the chestnut on a piece of string about one foot in length. I watched how my classmates looped the other end of the string around their finger, drew back the chestnut, then bashed as hard as they could against the other lad's chestnut, trying to split it open.

Brownie, my chestnut, was the toughest chestnut in Scotland, I was sure, ready to take on all comers, if they'd just let me play. "You're a weakly little Yank," they said, striding off to play under the great chestnut tree.

I watched and waited. I polished Brownie and practiced by myself, aiming at the stub ends of pencils I swung from strings in my bedroom. My aim got better. My strike grew harder. Day after day, I took Brownie to school with me, waiting for a chance. With Brownie in my pocket, I felt a little bigger, a little braver. Still, they wouldn't let me play.

Harold's chestnut had won thirteen straight. He was the indisputable champion. I thought about it for a week. He was standing out at the front bench when I approached him. "I've got a conquer ready to bash."

Harold barely looked up. "Take yer wee conquer and run back to yer mum, would ya now."

"You afraid?" I said.

"Afraid?" he sneered. "Of a bloody Yank? Never."

"Then let's ha' it out." I tried my best to sound Scottish.

"I'll bury ya," he said. "So deep yer mum'll n'er find ya. Out at the tree. Thursday, after school." He swung his satchel over his shoulder and left.

Wednesday night I spent an hour polishing Brownie with an extra layer of dark brown shoe polish. Thursday I thought of nothing but the coming battle. Brownie waited in my pocket. I whispered to him. "You can do it, lad, I know you can."

Ten other boys, sweaty and jeering, gathered under the chestnut tree to witness the clash. "Bash him, Harold. We're with ya, lad." My cheering squad was more modest: me. And Brownie.

Harold and I measured off, ten paces between us. We circled round each other. Harold's chestnut was almost twice the size of mine. "Don't look at him," I whispered to Brownie.

Harold twirled his chestnut wide then swooped in from the left. Crack—a direct hit. "Smash 'em, Harold." I tried to block out the chants. "HAR-LLD! HAR-LLD!" Harold swooped back in. Another smash. Brownie had never been hit so hard. The pencil stubs didn't hit back. A small crack opened on one side.

I backed away, a chance to take a breath. The lads taunted me. "Yankee, Yankee, lookin' for his hanky." Now I was mad. We cracked and smashed. Harold smacked Brownie twice, but we got in a quick rebound blow. The chorus chanted, "Go! Harold, Go!" Harold looked over, winked at them, a smug smile. I saw my chance, launched Brownie, as fast and hard as I could, scored a direct hit. Pieces of chestnut flew. I wasn't sure who had cracked, Harold's chestnut or Brownie. I heard the lads mumbling among themselves. Calhoun came running over. "Am I too late? Is the Yank on his knees yet?"

I looked down at Brownie. Still with me, spinning, dancing on the end of his string. Custom was for the loser to offer the broken pieces of his chestnut to the winner. I waited for Harold, but Harold kicked his broken pieces, his chestnut shattered beyond recognition.

Brownie and I stood off to the side, watching. Harold turned to face me. "Ye're just a bloody Yank, y'are, a wee bit daft an' no so swift a runner neither. I did'na bring my best chestnut, 'cause you're no worthy of it, so don' ye' go bein' so full of ye'self."

Harold walked away. The other lads followed, leaving Brownie and me alone. I slipped him into my pocket. On the way home, I polished him, rubbed his wounds. "You're the best, Brownie. Don't listen to what Harold says." I wanted to put Brownie someplace special, so I would always remember him, but where? I slept with him under my pillow, my hand curled around him.

One day I knelt down by the flower bed along the edge of the house and dug a hole. I said a quick prayer, laid Brownie in the dirt, poured some water over the hole, and whispered to him, "One day, Brownie, you'll be father to the toughest chestnuts in all of Scotland."

I visited him, and watered him daily. "Now grow!" I commanded. "Brownie, please grow." I waited and watched. Nothing. Then more nothing. My doubts grew, but no Brownie.

Three months later, I was in the garden with Dad, watching his trowel thunk in the rocky soil, fresh, new life everywhere. The breeze gathered; long shadows crept across the lawn. We'd been working in silence for ten minutes, when Dad exclaimed, "Look at this! It's a bloody horse chestnut." He banged Brownie with his trowel, then tossed him in the weed pile.

"That's Brownie!" I trembled. "Put him back in the ground, please."

Dad shook his head, kicked dirt over the hole. "If that thing grows, it'll knock the house down."

"Brownie's not a thing. You can't throw him away." I picked up Brownie, admired the stalk, six inches or more, growing directly out from the crack he split open in the fight with Harold.

Dad kneeled down next to me. "Let me see that."

I held Brownie in my hand. Dad reached out to touch

him. I could almost feel Brownie growing. The three of us stood so close together, I could smell Dad's sweet pipe tobacco. I watched the smoke curl around Brownie.

"We have to plant him back in the ground. So he can grow."

Dad nodded. "Far from the house."

We found a place up near the gooseberry bush. I dug a hole. Dad poured some water in. We placed Brownie and the fresh, green sprout that was growing out of him carefully in the hole, filled in the soil, and tapped it all around. Dad sat, uncharacteristically silent and still, and stared at Brownie for a long time, as if waiting for the chestnut to grow. "Not even Brownie will grow that fast," I joked.

"No, but you will," he said.

Chapter 4

It's four in the afternoon when I arrive for my weekly visit at Chapin Hospital. It's been four months since Charlie and I first met. I give up trying to convince him to talk. I want to see him, that's all. Something is missing in him. Something is missing in me too. Maybe we can help each other. Mildred tolerates my visiting him. "Don't say I didn't warn you," is all she says.

I've developed a special rat-a-tat-tat knock to announce my arrival. Charlie never responds, but I like to imagine he knows it's me. When I open the door, he's still in his pajamas. "Hi, Charlie. You didn't have to get dressed just for me." I've started kidding him a bit, like this. I imagine he enjoys it, but I don't really know. I play as if we're buddies. I tell him about my classes, the terrible food in our dining hall, and my new girlfriend, Peggy. I prattle on. "Getting cold these days, down into the teens last night. I have a test in US history tomorrow, haven't even done the reading yet. Our football team lost again, 33–3 this time. What do you do with a football team that loses 33–3?"

After fifteen minutes, I run out of chatter. Charlie, as usual, hasn't said a word, but I'm okay with that. I head for the door, but sense him standing, then approaching me from behind. Mildred's "Danger!" warnings thwack in my brain. He is, after all, one of "them." I turn, ready. I've always thought of him as huge, but he looks smaller now. Maybe I've grown accustomed. He stretches out his hand, as if he's reaching for something, squints, parts his lips slightly. He's missing a front tooth, lower left side. The first sound out of his mouth, a long, deep bass groan, ohhhhhhhh, rises like a sound from the crypts of a medieval monastery where it's languished for centuries.

I freeze, waiting to see if he'll make another sound. When I look into his eyes, all I see is the reflection of my own demons. His breath dwindles, and the moan fades. The next voice I hear is soft, but the words are clear. "I know…" he pauses—long enough to let a generation pass—"what it's like to lose."

The pain of what he's saying whispers through me. The joy of his speaking stretches into a mile-wide smile across my face. I want to run into the hallway and yell it out for all to hear, "Charlie spoke! He spoke!" I play it cool. "Yeah, me too," I say.

"I played ball in school," he says.

"I figured you might have. What position?"

We exchange a few more sentences. Football. Life. He paces about the room, sweeps the lock of hair off his forehead, sits back on his bed. I smile. We sit for a while, let the silence wash over us. "I like when you visit," he says. "Will you come back?"

"I will," I tell him. "You bet I will."

Before I leave the hospital, I tell Mildred about our conversation. She looks at me, dubious. "Thank you. I'll note that in his chart."

On the way home, I ponder my time with Charlie. How did it happen? He is surrounded by mental-health professionals. I am a first-year psych student. I know nothing about mental health, and yet he opened up, for the first time…to me. Why? I didn't know anything about his illness, so I saw him as a person. I had no pills to give him, so I gave him a little bit of time and attention. I stay with the wonder for a few moments, until a different, louder voice drowns out the first. I did nothing. It means nothing. He spoke, but that was coincidence. It could have been anyone. I happened to be there. It's no big deal.

Or is it?

I decide at the end of freshman year that I don't, after all, want to work in mental health. But Charlie's image— his shy lock of jet-black hair, his missing tooth, that long "ohhhhhh," his voice, after years of silence, "I know what it's like to lose"—is wrapped like a Red Cross flag around my heart. I try to make sense of our "friendship." How can it be? A little miracle.

The last time I visit Charlie is just before the end of freshman year. He's no longer just a mental patient I'm visiting. We've become friends. He talks now, full sentences, and even smiles sometimes. I feel awkward, knowing our relationship is about to end. As I stand to leave, he surprises me. "I won't forget you."

Tears well inside me. I squeeze them down. *Real men don't cry.* I turn away, but half out the door, I feel his hand on my shoulder. "I'll repay you someday." It's an intriguing comment, particularly coming from a man of such few words as Charlie. I dismiss it quickly as words that people say but don't mean. How could I know these were among the most prophetic, most meaningful words I had ever heard?

✳

I spend most of the first two years of college wandering aimlessly from this class to that, this girl to that, fantasies of this career or that without ever really investigating or thinking about any of them, skimming the surface, too fearful to dive down deep, because down there lurking underneath it all is the question, who am I? Unanswerable, except for the non-answer: I am the pleaser. I am the doubter. I am whoever *they* see me as. I am the big nothing.

In high school, I tried desperately to be cool. In college, everyone wants to be a hot shit. To be a shit used to be bad, but now it's good—so long as it's hot. The absurdity of it all makes me laugh. The reality of my failures makes me cry.

My one diversion from my plodding academic approach is a creative writing class, taught by the novelist John Hawkes. I tiptoe into class and sit in the back. Professor Hawkes is the kind of man, the kind of writer, I yearn to emulate. His encouragement could lift me out of my well of insecurity; his criticism could drown me forever.

Our first major assignment is due. I clear my desk, water the plants, make coffee, and roll a sheet of paper into my blue portable Olivetti typewriter, a high-school graduation present from my parents. I'm ready to write. The paper stares at me, expectantly. Where are my notes? Where is my research? Blood drains from my face. My hands tremble. Without reference books, I have no idea where to begin. I go to the bathroom, clean the sink, pop a pimple. I signed up for this class because I wanted to try my hand at something creative, but as the moment descends, doubt rises up in front of me. "Study the issue." That's what I learned in high school. That's what my fears tell me. "Pull up your socks." That's what Mom told me. "Listen to what your teachers are telling you." I type one and a half sentences before ripping the paper from my typewriter. I check the clock. It's past midnight. The paper is due in nine hours. I change into my pajamas. Stare at the page. Still empty. I pace the room. Get more coffee. It's two o'clock. My heart races. What do people write about anyway? I grab random books, open to random pages, rummage for random ideas. I'll write about anything: my pajamas, the weather, the party I went to last weekend, my mother's girdle. I don't care. Anything. Just to get words on the page. Three a.m. Two wretched sentences stare cross-eyed at me.

I could get sick. I could drop the class. Drop school. Join the army.

I make a vow. I will write the first thing that comes into my mind, regardless of how inane it might be. I won't hesitate. I will write.

I glance at my coffee cup. A few drops of coffee languish in the saucer. A tiny bubble forms between the cup and the saucer, daring me. I try to stare it down. It mocks me. I should be writing. Why am I wasting time with this bubble? I vowed to write about the first thing that entered my mind, but you can't write about a bubble. I slam the coffee cup, try to squash it, but the bubble reappears on the other side of the cup. I'll write about my rage. Rage at the bubble. The bubble cackles. We face off. A surge of pique, and my fingers fly across the keyboard. Thrust, parry, feint to the left, duck, hide, swing, write. We are locked in battle. I type without censor. Words and images, thoughts and feelings spew across the page. It is terrible, but there are words on the page. I title it "The Worst Story Ever." Then I change the title to "Me and the Bubble." I slam shut my typewriter and fall into bed.

I stumble into class and slip "The Bubble" to the bottom of the pile on Mr. Hawkes's desk, then retreat glumly to the rear. I'm no writer.

One week later, I'm back in class, in time to catch Professor Hawkes waving my bubble story like a flag on the Fourth of July. I smell his disgust. He's going to roast me. I'd escape, but he's already closed the door. I sink as far down in the chair as I can, stare at the floor, build a wall of books on the desk in front of me, gird myself for humiliation.

Mr. Hawkes rests his green book bag on the desk, removes his owl glasses. "One paper from the last assignment stood out because of its raw, fresh honesty. I'd like to read it."

A moment of reprieve. Then horror again. *He's going to read something good, then mine, to show the chasm between.* But goose bumps pop on both arms as Professor Hawkes reads the opening of "Me and the Bubble." He stops. "Listen to how this language puts you inside the author's experience. How you can feel the author's desperation. How the scene propels the reader forward, eager to know how this situation will resolve."

Professor Hawkes has misjudged. I did nothing except to give in meekly to my desperation. I sink into my chair, ambushed into stunned silence. It is the last paper of mine my teacher reads. After this experience, I stick to what others have thought and said, digested and regurgitated, the ordinary, the predictable, the boring. I get a B in the class and consider myself lucky. I never take another creative writing class.

*

Why do failures—and perceived failures—burrow into the psyche with such ease, taking up residence, like moles who've established a network of tunnels undermining the garden before you're even aware of their presence; while successes, equally real but ephemeral as last night's dreams, scamper off into hiding? I have a theory: for so many years, our ancestors struggled day and night for survival. One little mistake meant the end. In modern times, we've evolved to a different state of being with our fancy cars and our high performance neocortexes. But a significant part of our brain still operates from the outdated reptilian model, seeing threats everywhere, fight or flight our only options. We— or at least I—seem so often stuck in a way of thinking that became outdated a few hundred million years ago. I'll catch up some day.

I make no connection between my experience with Charlie and my writing about the bubble. I realize nothing about the significance of these events, or how the seeds might have been planted years earlier, when I was a small boy, learning, supposedly, how to be me in the world. It never dawns on me that these two events are stops on a journey down a crooked path that I will travel for decades, unsure where the path is leading, or if it is leading anywhere at all.

*

The university cafeteria (official name the refectory, but referred to, though not in any relation to Wally's experiment, as the "rat factory") is a large square building with kitchen and serving lines in the middle. I stand in line, tray in hand, three times a day, my mind still churning about the rats in Professor Temple's classroom. I wait dumbly for my pellets, eat, then go to class. It is what I am conditioned to do.

Surrounding the food service area is a huge dining space filled with tables for eight. The rat factory feeds mostly the male students. Female students have their own dining hall at Pembroke College. They show up occasionally at the rat factory, always with an escort. As for the food, what I remember best is the sticky smell of the Sunday cinnamon buns, a plump wheel of fresh dough, glazed with a thick sheet of melted sugar, topped with a generous slab of butter, sized for giants.

As I enter the rat factory, my eyes scan hundreds of sleepy, hungover eyes, ragged jeans, unwashed bodies, unshaven faces. I stumble past a table with a cinnamon bun, just one bite gone, then abandoned. From the plate of an overstuffed rat, I assume. At the same moment that I see this bun, I spot Carolyn, the redhead with freckles from Professor Temple's class, and a member of the badass psychologists team, whom I've dated a couple of times. She is holding hands with a guy, no one I know, heading toward the food service area, like all the other rats. What happens next was, and is, a jumble in my mind. Though I have no memory of ever making a decision, I launch into action. Call it a conditioned response, if you like. I grab the cinnamon bun from the table and hurl it, as hard as I can, at

Carolyn. I am no star outfielder with a bull's-eye throw to the plate, but I score a lucky, perfect strike. Although she is at least five tables away, the bun splats her cheek. I watch her startle, then freeze, then reach to protect her face.

I drop my tray and slink out the door in horror, embarrassed, as confused as I imagine she must be. Did anyone see me? Might they tell her who it was? Will word spread? Will there be stories in the student newspaper: "The Mystery of the Disappearing Bun Tosser; Was He Aiming at Her?" "Can You Hit a Moving Target 50 Feet Away with a Cinnamon Bun?" "Random Bun Pitch Inspires Bun-Throwing Contest in Refectory." For me, it's first about the fear of being discovered. Fear morphs into shame, then sadness. She might have been my girlfriend. Why didn't I pursue her more? I was attracted, but she seemed out of my league. I doubted. So why this senseless…?

I spot Carolyn around the campus, but I avoid contact, never confess, never even speak to her again. Instead of taking appropriate action (such as apologizing, which I never even consider), I turn my shame inward and find a waiting reservoir of self-disgust. I ponder. I churn. I burrow down. I obsess over how the same guy who had seemingly grasped the power of kindness with Charlie could perpetrate something as mean and destructive as what I did to Carolyn. Self-doubters and idealists don't remain strangers for long. Who am I, anyway?

I think again about Professor Temple and the rats. I learned something about psychology, not much about humanity.

Chapter 5

Rushing in from the garden to our dining room in Scotland, I announced, "Brownie comes up to my ankle already."

Mom gave me the who-is-Brownie look.

"Brownie, you know, my chestnut tree. He's going to be bigger than the house, and he's going to make the best, toughest chestnuts in Scotland."

"That's nice." Mom reached over to grab my plate. "More noodle kugel?" I shook my head, got up from the table, eager to be back in my own world. "I'm going to put on my kilt."

"But you like noodle kugel."

I was already on the third stair when Mom's words sliced through me. "I gave your kilt away. Boys in America don't wear kilts."

Gave my kilt away? She can't…I ran up the stairs to my room, first on the left, and turned the handle. The door was locked. It had never been locked before. Back downstairs, Mom was in the living room, in front of the fireplace, with Virginia. "Why is my door locked?"

"Sit down."

"Why is my door locked?"

Mom rubbed her hands together, paced back and forth.

"There are a lot of things you're too young to understand yet."

"I'm six years old."

She sat down, stared into the fireplace. "It's time you knew. We're going back to America. I've been clearing up your rooms, packing your things. The house has been sold. You'll both sleep downstairs for a few days, until we leave."

"You can't take my kilt. I'm staying here with Brownie. I'm Scottish. I'm not American."

Mom poked the fire. "America is so much warmer than here. You'll have all the eggs and chocolate milk you want. And the ice cream is so much better than the frozen water they sell here. You can roller-skate to Sheridan Circle, and you can wear long pants to school. You'll love Washington, and we'll go up to Blue Ridge in the summer, and—"

"I won't go."

"Where will I go to school in Washington?" Virginia asked. She didn't care about Scotland. "Where will we live?"

"We'll live with Mayma and Grandpa."

I smelled the sweet, familiar aroma of Dad's pipe. He was leaning against the doorway. I turned to hear what he'd say, but he wasn't looking at me. Or Virginia. He was looking into the fire. Virginia asked him, "Will you take your pilot training school with you to Washington?"

Dad inspected his pipe as if the answer might be mixed in with the tobacco. Virginia's question floated in the air. Mom lit a cigarette, then blew out the match and tossed it in the fireplace. "Daddy is staying in Scotland. For now."

Maybe Virginia understood, but it took me a while. "I want to stay here too. Why is Dad so lucky?"

Mom stood up, poked the fire once more, then left the room without answering my question.

After dinner, Virginia and I sat alone in the living room by the fire. The fire was the only light in the room, worms of flickering light that wiggled up the walls. Mom went upstairs to finish packing. "You two stay down here. I'll call you when it's time for bed."

I was playing with a truck. Virginia had her dolls. The fire was dying. I zoomed my truck away. "It's getting cold."

"Poke it," Virginia said.

"Not allowed to."

"You're scared." She put down her doll and went over to the fire tools, the poker, the shovel, the brush, each with a long, shiny brass handle, keepers of the flame, like the guards who stood still as statues and all serious on the stone steps in front of the big buildings in Edinburgh. Virginia stirred the logs with the poker. A bigger flame reflected in her eyes. A little extra warmth was always welcome. "When you poke the logs hard, like this," she said, "they throw out sparks, like stars. You try."

"I'm not allowed to touch the fire."

"They're upstairs." She poked the logs again. More stars. "They won't know." A big piece of log broke off. I could feel the extra heat warm my face. Virginia pulled the poker out of the fire and offered it to me. "Here."

"No."

"You're scared."

"I'm not scared. I'm tough." Impulsively, I reached out to grab the poker. She withdrew it. Now I wanted it. She put the poker back in the stand. "You poked the log. Why can't I?"

"You're too young."

"I'm six years old."

"Maybe when you're seven."

"Six is old enough."

"Just once." She withdrew the poker from its rack, held the brass handle and pointed the black tip toward me. "See if you can make the stars jump."

I looked into the fireplace. I won't leave Scotland. I won't go. They can't make me. They don't even wear kilts in America. Then an even worse fear invaded. "They play bagpipes in America, don't they?" I asked Virginia.

"I don't think so."

"They must play bagpipes. I'm going upstairs to ask."

"They told us to stay downstairs, remember?" She held the handle and pointed the working end of the poker at me again. "A big boy knows how to poke a fire. If you poke hard enough, you'll make stars."

I'll show her.

Thinking about the stars, I grabbed the red-hot end.

Pain seared through my fingers, my palm, up my arm. My fingers gripped tighter. The pain dug deep into my hand, then balled up in my stomach. From deep in my gut, a long, agonized, "Aaaaaah."

"Let go. Let go!" Virginia yelled. I tried. I couldn't. I couldn't open my fingers. The smell of burning flesh smothered my screech. My skin was welded to the poker. I screamed again, louder and again. Virginia raced to the door, yelled upstairs. "Come down. Quick. Peter burned himself. Come!" Mom was at the door. She grabbed my hand, "Drop it! Drop it."

But the poker and my hand had become one. "Water," Mom shouted. "Get some water. Quick."

They threw water over my hand as I screamed. Steam curled around my fingers. The smell of burning flesh everywhere. Mom tried to peel one of my fingers away. I clenched tighter. A strip of skin pulled away from the bone, like a strip of bark. "Let go. Let go, you have to let go." *I can't let go.* The harder she tried to open my fingers, the tighter I gripped. The stench, like rotting…that's me. Ridges, valleys of black and red, parched, me…not me…pieces peeling like strips of old glue, not me, not possibly me. Me. The room…dimmed…the pain fading…darker…to black. I was floating. White walls. White sheets. White bandages on my hand. A man in a white coat. A woman holding my arm. Mom at the end of the bed. Dad, his hand on my leg. Until everything went blank again.

Chapter 6

At the start of college, I attend Catholic Mass regularly. I was raised Catholic, attended a Catholic school, and at one time seriously considered becoming a priest. Then I start missing, too hung over. I'm drinking more, enjoying it less, drinking for the effect, drinking to be cool, drinking to cover the doubt. Some Sunday mornings, I join the hungover crowd, downstairs in the fraternity basement that smells eternally of stale booze and cigarettes, where we tell tales of the outrageous things we did the night prior. "I was so shitfaced I couldn't remember her name," Mike says.

"You were passed out on the couch at eight o'clock."

"I stopped counting after my tenth vodka Coke. Very disappointing. I wanted to make it to twelve." Everyone trying to one-up the last wild story. I listen. I nod. I smile, as if I am enjoying it. I have my own stories, but I prefer to keep them to myself.

I avoid church. But one Sunday, as I slump in my pew, I am aware that I've been listening to the priest drone on for twenty minutes. My body is there, but my spirit is missing. I am bored. I gaze at the statues of saints. They offer me no hope, they hold me in no fear. They are painted idols, nothing more. I ask myself why I am there. The answer is obvious. I am in church out of habit and because, years ago, I learned—I was conditioned—to be afraid of going to Hell. But I no longer believe in Hell. Hell is a myth, a useful way for the church to control me. I don't need to be afraid of Hell any longer.

The priest rambles on, tired echoes of a message I once believed, but now scoff at. "Sinners. Alcohol is the drink of the devil. Satan awaits you."

It happens so quickly, as impulsive as throwing the bun. I stand, drop my missal on the seat behind me, and shout out, "Hell is here. Right here."

The priest glowers down from the pulpit, like a politician facing a heckler. What's he to do, throw me out? I babble on about God and Satan and Professor Temple and rats and conditioned reflexes and cinnamon buns. I don't know what I'm saying, but the words keep coming. The girl in the pew in front turns and scowls. A girl to my left tries to pull me back down. "Stop it. You're in church. You're embarrassing everyone."

I can't stop it. It's not just Hell. It's God, too. God doesn't exist, except in our minds. But existence is in our minds. So if God is in my mind…? I create my thoughts. If I have free will. But I don't have free will. Even my thoughts are the products of my conditioning. So God is a conditioned response. Like everything. Or he is a product of my imagination, which is also a conditioned response. Soon the whole tent collapses. None of it makes any sense, whether I have free will or whether I'm a rat turd. I nod good-bye to the nudger next to me, climb over the others in my pew, glance one last time at the priest in the pulpit, turn, and leave the church, never to return again, except for weddings and funerals.

Whether it's too much drink or too little church, and whether Hell exists or not, whether I choose my behavior or whether I am a rat turd, my grades and my spirits droop in parallel. I go underground, like a prisoner on the run. I am the condemned and the condemner.

I drop out of my fraternity, abandon the varsity tennis team, and give up all physical exercise. I seek out the saddest songs and listen to them until I'm as blue as the lyrics. I move off campus into a dingy basement apartment that smells like mildew, one tiny window, caked with mud and cobwebs, the bathroom directly opposite the kitchen, designed so the smells can mix easily. Even as I sign the lease, I hear a voice shouting, "No!" But another, louder voice tells me I am a rat and this is where I belong. When I move in, I find a half-eaten ice cream sandwich in the freezer, otherwise a space that feels like it has never known life. Sometimes I bring home a bottle of cheap wine and sit, alone at the kitchen table, pouring and drinking in dribs and drabs until the bottle and I are done. Drifting off, I wonder how long it would be, if I died, before someone would realize. The smell, I suppose, would alert them. I hang one picture on the wall, a print from Picasso's blue period, a family at the beach, two parents and a young boy, could be the holy family, heads bowed, withdrawn and isolated, the adults especially, lost souls. They are my family. I spend hours sitting at the Formica table, staring at this picture. If I go out at all, I go to the library to study in the stacks, at a special metal desk I have selected, in a corner that has never, will never see light. Night after night, I lay my papers and assignments on the desk, then surrender to fatigue. I flop my head down on the desk and sleep until the library closes, when I wake up with a stomachache and a stiff neck. I trudge home, eyes lowered, head bowed, berating myself for one more wasted night.

I lie on the bed in my dark, damp basement, unsure if I am real or perhaps I am my own bad dream. Nothing is certain, except that I am weak. I doubt everything. I doubt my own existence. I hear my mother telling me to "Pull up my socks." I try, but my socks want to be down. It is the time of the Cuban missile crisis. Everyone talks and worries about nuclear annihilation, a subject worthy of worry, but my concerns are closer to home: do I dare put on my pants? Can I summon the strength to open a can of tuna? Dust motes of doubt, neither noble nor tragic, just petty and paralyzing. Weak, I am weak.

Eventually I fall asleep, then awaken to the realization that I am still alive, still me, one more day in my own skin. I lecture myself on how I've been given so much and wasted it. I am worthless, incompetent, broken, mired in the thick goo of self-judgment. I try to hide how desperate I am. Surely everyone sees it. They know. They laugh. I imagine them shaking heads and wagging fingers, talking about me behind my back. Shame climbs all over me. I should be able to snap out of it. I live inside the double wammo: feeling guilty, and feeling guilty about feeling guilty.

I think back to Wally's experiment. I remember his look of satisfaction when he declared that I was a rat. He is right. I am a rat. As long as I run in the rat race, I will be a rat. I feel a tiny shift, a recognition that a certain amount of disappointment in life is inevitable, but misery is optional.

Despite Wally's experiment, I know I have a choice. So why am I incapable of making it?

Looking back, the symptoms of depression are obvious. Back then, the word "depression" barely appeared in the dictionary. I was a late model car that should be cruising down the highway, but in fact I was sputtering in a ditch. I knew I should be able to get out of the ditch, to shake this…whatever it is. I have a choice, but I can't choose.

I conclude that something is seriously off about me. I don't know what to call it. I am a rat. I eat my little pellets and dwell in darkness.

Chapter 7

My hand like a charred piece of coal, we delayed the return to America. I refused to—or I couldn't—open my fingers. Weeks after the incident, I could still feel the searing hot poker. Miss MacDougal worked with me every day, inventing little games for my fingers to play. She opened and shut my hand, but the hand was like a claw, spring-loaded. Mom was crying when I overheard them talking. "With regular therapy, perhaps for years, he may regain use of the hand," Miss MacDougal said.

Mom worked with my hand twice every day. One finger at a time. A few degrees open, shut, open. Then the next finger. And again. I didn't fight the sessions any more. I got a lot of attention. No one else had a hand like mine. The lads at school all wanted to see it. I told the story again and again.

"Did it hurt?"

"Sure."

"Did you cry?"

"No."

When Mom worked on my hand, Virginia had to sit still and be quiet. I liked that.

Dad had been gone for a couple of days when Mom sat us down on the couch in the living room, Virginia on one side, me on the other. "We're leaving for America in two weeks," she said. "Scotland is so backward. They have all the latest techniques and medicines in America. They will fix your hand, and then you'll learn to play baseball."

*

I stared out the window of the plane and watched the clouds fly by. "When is Dad coming to America?" I asked.

Mom reached across me. "Fasten your seat belt."

"Why isn't he here?"

"Would you like to read your Babar book?" Mom wore her favorite worried expression. I wondered what I'd done wrong. "Babar is for babies."

"Here, look at this, then." She put a magazine in my lap and turned to Virginia.

I asked about Dad a few times and then stopped asking. A new friend appeared in my mind. I named him Scotty, and he instantly became my best friend.

I talked about everything with Scotty. "Dad will come to America soon, Scotty." Scotty didn't say much, but he was a good listener. "We're going to plant a chestnut tree, Scotty, and I'm going to teach all the boys how to play conquers." Scotty nodded again. He thought that was a good idea. I don't remember much more about Scotty, except that he was the only person I felt I could talk with and be myself. No pretending. No worry. No hiding. So sweet. One day Scotty disappeared. It was years before I found anyone to replace him.

The plane bounced about, and I felt sick. Mom held my sick bag in front of me. I threw up, but Virginia didn't. Scotty went with me to the bathroom to help me clean up. The plane smelled bad.

We stopped to refuel in Iceland, which was a big disappointment—not made out of ice at all.

The next thing I remember was looking out the window as we descended into Washington. The plane flew so low, I could see people in their gardens with barbeques. I could almost smell the meat. It made me hungry. Maybe they don't have kitchens in America, I thought, but Mom said they have everything in America. The houses looked huge. Some kids were tossing a big brown egg back and forth. I was sure they'd drop it and the egg would break.

"Why are they throwing that brown egg?" I asked mom.

She leaned over me to look out the window and laughed. "That's not an egg. It's a football."

Mom didn't know much about sports. "A ball is round," I told her.

"A football is oval, like a big egg," she said.

I wasn't about to accept that. I'd played football in Scotland. That is, I'd swung my leg at a ball, and I knew the ball was round. "A football is round," I said again, louder this time, but mom shook her head. We argued back and forth until a man from across the aisle leaned over. "They're playing what we call 'football' in America. You throw the ball, like they're doing down there. The game you call football, we call soccer."

What a strange country, this America. They throw a football, instead of kicking it, and the ball is egg shaped, not round the way a ball is meant to be, and then they call it "sock her," which is a very silly name for football, especially because girls don't even play. I'm not so sure about this America. I miss Scotland, bagpipes, and Brownie.

Chapter 8

Somehow, I pass my classes and stumble through the Van Wickle gates to receive my college diploma, then fall into a job with the state department, to work in a binational center in Lima, Peru. Realizing how messed up I am myself, I have long since abandoned my original idea of becoming a psychiatrist. I've glommed on to the idea of Foreign Service. I've been reasonably successful in French. I grew up in an international environment. I know how to smile and please others. What else is required for a diplomatic career?

I arrive in Lima and share a house with Tony, a friend from Brown, who has a similar job, though in a different center in a different part of the city. Tony was a Spanish major and speaks perfect Spanish. I speak only the few words I cram into my head in the short time between graduation and arrival in Lima. But I am determined to learn, and commit myself to speaking nothing but Spanish once I get to Peru.

A few days after arrival, I am part of a Lima lunch party, about ten of us, all Peruvians plus me, so the lively, social banter is all in Spanish. I understand 2 percent, but I practice repeating these strange new sounds in my head and throw in an occasional "*por favor*," and "*no entiendo, pero estoy aprendiendo español.*" (I don't understand, but I am learning Spanish.) After an hour of gossip and food, it's time to order dessert. Ordering food is the right level challenge for me. I plan out my sentence, making up right-sounding Spanish where I don't know the word. The waiter stands, pen in hand, behind me."*¿Señor, que quere usted?*" (What would you like, sir?)

Uncharacteristically bold, I'm up for this challenge, I boom out my reply. "*Me gustaría caca de chocolate, por favor.*" (I'd like chocolate shit, please.)

The table falls silent. All eyes swivel toward me. Bashed by the club of doubt, I feel the hot blood pool at my face. I am an international disgrace. That night, I redouble my commitment to Spanish. No more caca.

✳

Violetta works as an office assistant in the binational center. Her sweet smile and patience with my bungling Spanish endear her to me. She dresses, always, in the same black top and skirt, black stockings, and black shoes. It's an unusual style, but her wardrobe next to her bone-white skin and ink-black hair is stunning. I hang around her far more than is necessary for the job. She's not that busy and doesn't seem to mind. One day, when my Spanish is up to it, as we stand by the window, l suggest a walk in the park.

Her dark eyes grow bigger. "*Me gustaría, pero no puedo.*" (I'd like to, but I can't.)

"Why not?"

She twiddles her black skirt. "*Estoy de luto.*"

It takes me some time to figure out this new phrase, "*de luto.*" Finally, I get it. "Oh, you're in mourning."

"*Si, si.*"

I learn that her grandmother died recently. "That's why I wear all black. I am not permitted to do anything social for six months."

I plan to be in Peru for a year. I can't wait six months. I press my case. "It is forbidden," she says.

I try to be understanding, but the custom rubs me all wrong. "You're twenty-five years old. You're alive. How does your staying home help your dead grandmother?"

Violetta is silent for a moment. "It's our custom." She looks down. I want to grab and ravish her, there in the office. Probably not a good diplomatic move. I take a step closer to her, let out an unintended sneer. "It makes no sense."

"We are different from you *norteamericanos*." Her hand shakes. She retreats from the window. "*No puedo*."

There is a strain between us in the office. Her tone is more formal. I let my eyes bathe in her beauty for longer. She looks away quicker. I ask her to reconsider. "*No puedo*," she says over and over, but I hear longing in her voice, or at least in mine. I persist.

A few weeks later, we are working late. Everyone else has left the building. "I should go home now," she says.

"We're almost finished. Can you help me sort through this one file?"

She weighs my request, runs her hand through her hair, lowers the black sleeves of her sweater, then nods.

"Thank you."

I watch the corners of her lips turn up. We start sorting the file. I bring her over a chair and she sits, her jet-black skirt slightly above her knee. I wait for her to pull it lower, but she doesn't. We are quiet for a while, then she asks me, "Do you have a girlfriend? In America."

It's the first personal thing she has ever asked. When she looks at me, her eyes rest on mine, seconds only but longer than ever before. My heart quickens. I lean forward. I think about the girlfriends I have had back home. "No. Not now."

She nods and reaches for the papers on the desk. She looks at me again, and this time her gaze lingers. My hand inches closer to hers. The Earth stands still. I wait to see. A tiny twitch of her eye. I close the gap between our hands. Rub mine, as softly as I can, across hers. I feel like I am holding a small bird. *Be careful, don't do any damage.* I touch her face. Her dark, chocolate eyes are steady. I draw her toward me. No resistance. Different from any kiss I've ever had in America. Soft kiss, gentle and delicate, lingering and sweet. We stand and embrace, rocking gently, then kissing again. Not a word. I wouldn't know what to say, in Spanish or in English. I am overcome by her tenderness. Happy. For the first time in so long, happy.

"I must go," she says. I don't argue. I ask if I can see her home. She frowns and shakes her head. "Not a word to anyone. Ever. Promise me!"

"I promise."

She is out the door. I close up, then skip home. In the morning, I come in early, putter about, on the lookout always for Violetta. She comes in late and seems to avoid me. All day, I try to get her attention. All day, she steers away from me. She leaves early without saying anything. The next few days, it's like a wall has gone up.

"Can I see you sometime?"

"*No puedo.*"

I buy a motor scooter. The first day after I register it, it's stolen from the driveway at work. I'm sure the former owner had a second key and drove it away. I go to the police. They laugh. Tony and I move to a new place. I take a trip, across the Andes to the jungle. When I return, I ask again.

"Can I see you?" She seems afraid of me. "I won't hurt you."

"*No puedo.*"

Jacques, a Swiss-Italian photographer friend, takes a portrait of me and presents it to me. The picture itself is out of focus. My eyes have a faraway expression, like I am contemplating hopeless existential issues, bathed in doubt, but it's a noble struggle. The photo becomes a symbol of that era and of what I both secretly like and fear in myself. I read and relate to Don Quixote, tilting at windmills. I set the picture on my bedside table and look at it often, just before I go to sleep. At least Don Quixote had real wind-mills, noble causes. My windmills are not noble. They're all in my brain. My insides are a hopeless yarn of guilt and shame, twisted into a big knot. I can't even articulate what I feel so badly about. *If only I had a reason for feeling bad. If I had some terrible disease, or had been badly abused. I feel bad about feeling bad. I want to be happy, but I'm sucked into the dungeon of doubt. Prisoner of my own deviled thoughts.*

After nine months, though I seem to have won the respect of my superiors, I am lonely and lost and filled with doubts about foreign-service work. I am filled with doubt about everything. Everything but one. It's been over three months since our brief romantic tease, but Violetta still invades my dreams.

Late one afternoon, when the center is quiet, I hear a quiet tap on my office door. "*Si, pasa.*"

Violetta approaches, close to the desk. "I have to talk to

you." Her voice, almost a whisper, is more somber than I've ever heard it before.

"Please sit. How are you?"

She doesn't sit. She looks away, tugs on her skirt. "I'm afraid," she says.

My mind searches. "Afraid? What are you afraid of?"

"What we did."

What is she talking about? I scan our history. Not much history to scan. "What did we do?" I ask.

"How long will it be?" she looks up at me, the way a young child might look at her mother.

"How long?" I repeat. "How long before what?"

"Before the baby."

Not just different countries. We live in different worlds.

Chapter 9

When we arrived in Washington after the flight from Scotland, we were met by a man in a dark blue suit and a cap, like the one Dad wore when he went off to fly. "I'm Barnes, ma'am." He tipped his cap to Mom. "Welcome to Washington."

I stared at Barnes. I'd never seen a man with such sunburned skin, like dark chocolate. Maybe even leather. I wanted to feel it and see if it was leather.

"Mom, why is Barnes—"

"Shhh."

I watched Barnes load our suitcases into a car four times the size of the car we had in Scotland, deep blue, with a black running board along each side and a shiny silver pelican hood ornament. We got in. The back seat was a living room. There was a glass partition between the back seat and the front. Barnes slid the glass open. He watched me watching him. "She's a Packard," he said. "Belongs to Mrs. Johnson, yo' grandma, where we're headin' now."

"Is Barnes a cousin?" I asked Mom.

"He's Mayma's chauffeur."

I didn't know what a chauffeur was, but I knew not to

ask. We were dripping in sweat. "You said we could get an ice cream when we got to Washington," Virginia said.

"Barnes, do you know an ice cream store anywhere nearby?" Mom asked.

"No, ma'am, but I'm sure there be one. I'll look around."

Ten minutes later, we were in the biggest store I'd ever seen, shelf after shelf loaded with candy, and a long counter on one side where people sat on stools licking strange-looking tennis balls, all colors, that they held on little tan pointed cups. Then they ate the cups.

Mom sat us down on stools at the counter. Barnes waited in the car outside. "What'll it be?" the lady behind the counter asked. I looked blankly at her. "We have any flavor you like," she said. "Chocolate, strawberry, raspberry, banana, pistachio. You name it. What'll it be?"

My eyes swam across buckets of different-colored ice cream. Scottish ice cream came in one color, and tasted like flavored water. We each got a cone, and Mom bought one for Barnes. I slurped and spread mine around my lips. For the first time, I understood about the cream in ice cream. Scotland began to fade.

In the car, Mom settled in the middle of the plush leather seat between Virginia and me. We drove down streets that were as wide as all of Ayr, past so many statues of men on horseback, under tunnels, and over bridges. The buildings were huge. Barnes parked the car in front of a hotel. "Here we are," he said, opening the car doors for us. "Mr. and Mrs. Johnson gon' be so excited to see you."

"What's that smell?" I asked Mom.

Mom frowned. "I think it's Barnes's cigar."

"He's not smoking a cigar," I said. We were parked in front of a brick building with bars on the windows. I'd never seen anything so tall. Other buildings were attached on both sides. In the front, there was a tiny square of concrete filled with pebbles. "Where's the house?" I asked.

"Right there," Mom pointed at the barred windows.

"Where's the grass?"

"Grass?" Mom repeated, as if she didn't know the word.

"Where do I play?"

"You'll learn to roller-skate." She rubbed her toe against the pavement. "Here, on the sidewalk."

The front door opened, and a lady with white hair, dressed in an ankle-length black dress, black ankle boots and a tight-laced collar, stepped out. I'd never seen anyone so old. "You're here at last." She spoke in a thin, birdlike voice.

Mayma bent low so Virginia and I could each give her a peck on the cheek. She wore thick, round magnifying glasses that made her eyes into huge, sea-blue circles. Behind her stood an old, bald man, in a dark suit, with a funny-looking ribbon tied in a bow around his neck. He stretched out his hand toward me. I looked up at him. "What's that bump on the top of your head?" I asked.

Mom grabbed my arm and tugged me away. "It's been a long trip," she said. "The children are tired."

"Is Grandpa's bump hard?" I asked Mom.

"Well, come in and sit down. Hattie's made some lemonade for you," Mayma said. She smelled like feathers.

The front hallway was dungeon dark. The house went up and up, four floors plus a basement. A huge grandfather clock stood guard at the top of the stairs, bonging out every hour. The big windows in the dining room and formal parlor on the second floor were covered with long, heavy drapes that were always drawn so the rooms were dark, with dark walnut knickknack cabinets covered by glass doors. The cabinets were loaded with tiny dolls and cups and teapots and plates and silver spoons and more things than we had in our whole house in Scotland. "Don't touch anything," Mom said.

There were so many rooms, I was afraid I'd get lost. I tried all the doors. Most of them were locked. Who lived in these rooms? It had to be ghosts. Uncle Willy was the first ghost I met, but he wasn't behind a locked door. He lived in the dining room, where a life-sized portrait in a gold frame stared down at me from the wall across from my place at the table. Uncle Willy was in army dress uniform, holding his plumed helmet in one hand, the other hand on his sword. His eyes were fierce, his black hair parted in the middle. He had a prominent mustache, like a handlebar with wings.

"Uncle Willy is your great-great uncle," Grandpa explained over dinner. "He joined the army, got a commission to go to West Point, but he didn't do his lessons. You have to do your lessons, you know. When Uncle Willy failed his exams, his mother, who was my stepmother, used her Washington connections to get him a direct commission into the US Army." By this time, I was pretty much bored and confused about what Grandpa meant by all the "great-greats" and whatever steps he was talking about, so I started pinching Virginia under the table.

"Pay attention when Grandpa speaks to you," Mom said.

I tried to focus on Grandpa. "Did he kill anyone with his sword?" I asked.

"Peter! Listen to the story."

"His mother pulled strings to get him assigned . . ." Grandpa continued.

I imagined a very old lady, maybe even older than Mayma, if that was possible, sitting with piles of string on a table. "Why was she pulling strings?" I turned to Mom.

"Hush. Listen to Grandpa's story. This is your heritage."

"She got Uncle Willy assigned to the prestigious Seventh Cavalry," Grandpa continued.

"What is per-stegion?" I asked, but no one was listening.

"Uncle Willy reported for duty three days before his regiment deployed to Wyoming to fight the Sioux," Grandpa continued.

"There's a girl named Sue in my class," I said.

"The Sioux Indians." Grandpa shook his head. "Uncle Willy's regiment was commanded by General George Armstrong Custer. Two weeks later, at the Battle of Little Bighorn, Uncle Willy was killed in what's now called Custer's Last Stand." Grandpa looked down. "His body was a pincushion of arrows."

"He was killed by the Indians?" I asked.

"The Indians killed every man there." Grandpa wiped his lips. "And every horse. Except one. One horse survived."

"Was Uncle Willy a cowboy?"

Grandpa frowned at me. "He was a brave soldier."

"But cowboys fight Indians." I looked over at Mom, hoping she'd explain.

"See what happens if you don't do your lessons," Grandpa said, as he stubbed out his Lucky Strike in the ashtray.

★

Mayma and Grandpa, Mom, and Virginia slept on the third floor. I slept on the fourth floor, which was originally for the servants, but there weren't any servants living there any longer, just a long corridor of locked doors.

At dinner, Grandpa tucked his napkin into his collar, like a bib, before he ate his pigs' feet. Pig's feet—yuck! I heard the bones crunch as he chewed. Then he pulled a piece of gristle from his mouth and left it sitting on his plate.

One day I overheard a conversation between Grandpa and Mom.

"You didn't run all over the house when you were growing up," he said. "Why can't you keep them quiet?"

"They're children, Father. They're bursting with energy." She paused. "Besides, you had governesses to help. I'm alone."

"Don't say I didn't warn you when you married him."

Mom's low sob ended the conversation. I wanted to comfort her somehow, but I didn't know how. "Children should be seen and not heard," Grandpa said.

"I don't think Grandpa likes me," I told Mom later. "I don't like him either."

She looked away. "Grandpa is a very distinguished man," she said. "He has met every president from Andrew Johnson through Herbert Hoover. He stopped when it came to Franklin Roosevelt, didn't want to shake hands with a traitor."

Before dinner every evening, Grandpa sat in his black leather chair next to the Philco table radio in the living room. As the news droned on, he blew a steady stream of smoke from his Lucky Strikes out toward the tasseled lampshade. Grandpa was seldom without a cigarette in his hand. The lampshade was covered in a grimy, brown film from all the smoke. The tips of Grandpa's fingers had turned yellow.

Mayma sat silently on the other side of the tasseled lampshade and took it all in through her thick glasses. She squinted and leaned her head to one side or the other, like she was maybe seeing something that others didn't see, then she called us over to her chair. The news over, it was her turn. She smelled like Juicy Fruit lozenges and had a tiny carpet of white peach fuzz that stretched across her chin and around her mouth. Virginia and I sat as close as we could so we could hear as she half sang, half recited a poem. Before she began, she'd take off her glasses and rub her eyes, exposing the little red spots on each side of her nose where her glasses pinched the skin. Then she began the poem about the demon butcher, Dunderbeck:

> Oh Dunderbeck, Oh Dunderbeck!
> How could you be so mean?
> I'm sorry you invented that terrible machine.
> No long tailed rat nor pussy cat will ever more be seen;
> For they're ground up into sausage meat in Dunder-
>   beck's machine!

Dunderbeck went on for many stanzas, climaxing when Dunderbeck climbed inside his machine to mend it. His wife "gave the crank, a heck of a yank, and Dunderbeck was meat!" Virginia and I shrieked with laughter and begged Mayma to recite Dunderbeck again, but she offered her cheek for a peck, whispered "Good night," and disappeared upstairs.

★

We were all at dinner one day. I was whining, desperate, miserable, pining for Jock, a large, Disney-type stuffy with teardrop eyes, that I'd spotted in a storefront window and fallen in love with. I talked about Jock and how he was going to come live with us. I absolutely and forever could not go on living without Jock, but the more I begged and pestered, the more fed up Grandpa was. And the more fed up Grandpa was, the more stressed Mom was. "Christmas will be here," she said. "If you still want Jock, maybe Santa Claus will bring him."

"Mind your mother," Grandpa said.

"Christmas takes forever," I said.

"Maybe for your birthday then," Mom said.

"Does my birthday come before Christmas? I can't wait."

"Eat your soup before it gets cold."

"Children have to learn to wait." Grandpa tossed his napkin on the table and stood to leave.

Mayma had been thinking. "Sometimes when you're six years old," she said, "you want something so badly, you can't wait."

That night when I went to bed, Jock was propped on my pillow, his big eyes staring up at me, exactly the way I'd seen him in the store window. I grabbed and hugged him to me. I crawled under the covers and took him down, into the darkness with me. "Jock, you're going to be my new best friend. And I'll tell you everything and you'll tell me everything." Jock agreed, and I was the happiest I'd ever been.

In the morning, I brought Jock to breakfast with me.

Grandpa said dolls didn't belong at the table. "He's not a doll," I protested. "He's Jock."

"Put him on the chair, under Uncle Willy," Mom said. "He'll wait for you there."

When Mayma came down, she looked at me, then over at Jock, then back at me. "Aha, he came," she said.

I nodded. I wanted to run over and hug Mayma, but you didn't do that kind of thing.

"You love that doll, don't you?"

I nodded again. Her kindness was a star in my sky, guiding me across the darkness, her smile quiet, deep, and warm, like a cup of hot chocolate waiting for me when I came in from the cold.

Chapter 10

It's 1971. I am twenty-nine years old, finishing my three-year tour with the US Air Force in Germany. I've enjoyed my time in Europe—learned to speak fluent German, acted in plays at bases across Europe, skied the Alps, and visited many of Europe's tourist attractions.

As my time in Germany draws to a close, I travel to Berlin to visit one of Europe's most iconic cities. I pause in awkward anticipation before the most famous wall in the world. Ice forms around my nose and mouth as I stand at Checkpoint Charlie, the border crossing between West Berlin and Communist East Berlin, the one place where I can—with the right documents and because of my military status—pass through the wall. *Why has mankind built so many walls for so many centuries? Walls to keep people out and walls to keep people in. Physical and metaphysical walls. Walls of stone, walls of language, of religion, of ethnic identity. Walls inside our cities; walls inside our minds.*

Walls separate good guys and bad guys, so I've been told. But I don't want to think like that. I want to open my mind wider. I want to cross through this wall and use my language skills to make real connection with East Germans.

"Something there is that doesn't love a wall." I remember "Mending Wall," Robert Frost's poem on the same subject. By the end of that poem, Frost had concluded, "Good fences make good neighbors." Was he right?

The sun is waking up. Dressed in my Air Force uniform as required by regulations, I button my heavy blue overcoat, tight to the neck. My thick long johns are no match for the cold that stabs into my fingers and toes. A somber young East German Grenztrupper (Border Police) with large, swimming-pool-blue eyes stands implacable at his post. I offer a weak smile, *"Ziemlich kalt heute morgen."* (Pretty cold this morning.)

"Why are you visiting the German Democratic Republic?" The air freezes his words in the space between us. Twenty-five yards away, more guards glare at me from their square, concrete block towers, fingers toggling the triggers of machine guns.

"I want to get to know East Berlin."

"East Berlin?" the boy-guard curls his lips around the sound. "There is no East Berlin. We are the capital of the German Democratic Republic."

Twenty seconds of conversation and already I've pushed the wrong button. Several smart-ass replies cross my mind before I review the guns around me and surrender. "I'm sorry, I—"

"You speak such good German. Your accent. How...?"

"Thank you, I work at it." Normally, I'm pleased to be complimented on my German, but this boy's voice smells of suspicion. He glances up at the guard tower. "Show me your identification."

A small, reddish pimple blushes at me from his left

cheek. I hand him my military ID. "Can you tell me where to get some breakfast?"

He tugs his cap lower over his forehead, waves me forward, and points down the street, the only direction possible from where we stand.

"*Danke.*" I weave around the heavy barriers set up on the Eastern side of the wall to halt anyone who might contemplate a dash to freedom. I'm reminded of the photos I've seen of East Germans trying to escape, machine gunned at the border. I step smartly, eyes straight ahead, hands clear of my pockets, heart on alert. The Berlin Wall, after all, is symbolic of the reason why we still have such a large military presence in Europe so long after the end of WWII. The Berlin wall has turned Eastern Europe into a prison yard, with Moscow as its warden. This wall is constructed from equal parts concrete, suspicion, and death.

Or am I falling into the kind of thinking I want to avoid, good guys and bad guys? Might there be another reality?

I step deeper into East Berlin, so different from the west. West Berlin became a rooster crow for democracy and capitalism after the war. Russia, by contrast, chose to suppress East Germany. East Berlin froze in time, as if the war had just ended, a portrait in dreary, a city of bombed-out buildings and people. East Berlin is filled with crumbling facades that line the empty streets, cookie-cutter, Soviet drab, windows and doors stacked like shoeboxes on a shelf. The few people I encounter scurry about, heads buried against the cold, eyes that scamper quickly away from mine. The women are all dressed in the same dingy, pale blue shapeless smocks. Smiles are out of fashion or not allowed. A mangy cat lets me pet her. Otherwise I am alone and disappointed. I want to move beyond Cold War politics and ideology. I want to connect across the web of our common humanity.

Our common humanity is on vacation. When I ask again about a place for breakfast, an elderly lady dressed, of course, in a faded blue sack, quivers and moves on without a word. I follow my guidebook to the Russian War Memorial, the cemetery, a few government buildings, the Lenin statue. I settle for a dingy storefront on Karl Marx Allee for lunch, where I am placed at a dingy table, where the waitress monotones in a dingy voice.

"What can you recommend?"

"Everything on the menu is good." She shrugs, hands me a menu, and withdraws.

I order the goulash, made from thin, dirty water left over perhaps from dishwashing. Maybe someone in the kitchen whispered "goulash" over it before it was served. A few elderly guests drop in for lunch. They cluster as far from me as possible. I wish I'd brought a peanut butter sandwich so I could sit in the park with the statues of happy socialist workers. The statues would be better conversationalists than the East Berliners I've encountered so far.

By midafternoon, I am done with East Berlin. Despite my efforts at conversation, no one speaks more than five words to me. I've seen nothing of interest or beauty, eaten nothing of taste or sustenance, experienced nothing but the dingy drudgery of life under a brutally repressive regime. I came in search of heart connection. Call me naive and foolish. I am ready for a hamburger and a Coke, ready to hear Carole King belt out "I feel the earth move under my feet." Ready for a smile.

I shamble along a tired street of late Stalin Sovietochek block houses. One lonely Trabant, the motorized wheelbarrow that is the pride of East German manufacturing, farts its way along, oil dripping from its tail. I decide to end my visit across town at the Brandenburg Gate, the most famous structure of Berlin. Ten minutes later, I stand in front of this eighteenth-century neoclassical arch, supposedly a monument to peace, but to my way of seeing, it exudes an aura of domination and control. Four horses and a charioteer look down from their pinnacle above twelve ultra-serious Doric columns. The gate was used as a symbol of the Nazi regime. "I am big, strong, and superior," the Brandenburg Gate says to me. "You are weak and insignificant."

Exactly how I feel.

Behind the gate, in the western sky, I glimpse the magnificent glow of the fading sun, swirling swaths of pink, crimson, and gold, beauty that dazzles and overwhelms me, lifting me momentarily out of my doldrums, reminding me of the beauty of our natural world and its power to liberate the human spirit. I stand in awe. But the long shadow of my day in East Berlin reminds me of how much of our pitiful human history has been consumed with suppressing, instead of liberating, the spirit.

I turn away from the sunset, trying to forget where I am, who I am, and even that I am, after all, an American GI, in uniform, in an "enemy" country. I close my eyes and feel a ball of sadness inside, rolling back and forth between what might be and what is. Good guys and bad guys. Walls everywhere.

I feel a faint tap on my left shoulder. Gentle. Almost imperceptible, and then a voice, "*Entschuldigung.*"

The sound is soothing. A hand rests on my arm. "Is it late?"

I turn toward the hand and notice an old, bent man with a white cane. He is still holding on to my arm as if trying to determine the perimeter of my being. "No, but the sun is setting," I tell him.

"Ahhhhh," he says, nodding and dragging out the sound, as if responding to some profound truth. "The sunset, is it pretty?"

"Yes, It's beautiful. Awe inspiring." He is almost a foot shorter than me, thinning hair, midseventies, I guess. The cuffs on his gray overcoat are tattered. He wears an armband on his left arm, three black globes on a yellow background, the European symbol for the blind. When he smiles, I can see his teeth, all asunder, like so many worn pebbles tossed in a bag. His balding head is bare. "Aren't you cold?"

"I walk here every day." He taps his cane a couple of times, then continues. "I haven't known you here before. Do you come often?"

"My first time ever in Berlin." He is the first East German to converse with me all day. As I contemplate why, the reason clobbers me: of course, he can't see the uniform. This totally blind man is the first person able to "see" me. "I've wanted to visit Berlin ever since I came to Germany."

"Ahhhhh." That same, long luscious sigh, like an early fall breeze, as if he wants to fully savor the sound. "Where are you from?"

I don't want to answer. We've only been talking for a few moments, but already I sense a kinship with this gentle man. Revealing my identity could kill any possibility for further connection. I could be from an Eastern-block country. Maybe I'd be Czech or Polish. But if I'm here seeking authentic connection, I have to own the truth. "I'm American," I mumble.

He shudders, moves back slightly. *Will he disappear like all the rest?* He shifts his weight from one foot to another. Then I realize something else. He knows I am American, but he doesn't know I am dressed in uniform, so he doesn't know that anyone watching us would also know that I am American. He doesn't run away. Rather he leaps like a kid let out of school early for a snow day. "American! Ahhhhh. Where? Where in America?"

"My parents live in Washington, DC. I don't know where I live anymore." I want to tell him why I am in Germany, why I am in East Berlin and how disappointing the day has been, that I've almost finished my time in the Air Force, that I am confused about what might come next. Instead I am silent.

"Washington. Such a pretty city." He touches my arm. I feel a wave shoot up to my shoulder. "The cherry blossoms are lovely."

"You've seen the cherry blossoms?" An elderly, blind East German talking about the beautiful cherry blossoms in Washington! Incredulity tugs at my sleeve.

"Seen them? No. But I've heard about them." A sardonic smile drops across his face. "Dieter told me about the cherry blossoms. He was in Washington. Only briefly. Some kind of secret talks over there. That's how it all started."

He is lost in memory. I feel like a swimmer who thinks he's in waist-deep water, only to discover he's been swept out to sea. I am bursting with questions. But before I can speak, he lobs another question at me. "You sound young. How old are you?"

"Twenty-nine."

"Twenty-nine!" He swallows hard. "Twenty-nine," he repeats. He takes my elbow. "There's a bench over there where I like to sit."

"I see it."

He nods toward the bench, a kind of invitation, before ushering me over. It's a short bench. We sit side by side, almost like lovers. His eyes are covered by thick dark glasses, but I can tell he is "looking" at something far away. "Dieter was twenty-nine," he says.

"Dieter?"

"My son."

"The one who was in Washington?"

He weaves his head to the left and right, the way blind people so often do, and rubs his hand across his thigh.

"Where is Dieter now?" I ask, and immediately wish I could take back the question.

When he speaks again, it is more a whisper, than a voice. "Dieter is dead."

He looks about, shifts awkwardly on the bench, looks like he might get up, then settles back down.

"I'm so sorry." I guess at it, but can't say what is on my mind. "Dieter was...sick?"

"Dieter was the healthiest one among us." He throws back his head, then lifts his cane like he might swat something with it, but then puts it back down. "He was shot. Trying to climb over the wall." He shakes the cane, then wiggles it again, for emphasis, I guess. "Shot," he repeats. "Trying to be free, like any normal young man."

A rustling alerts me to the trees behind us. *Is someone watching? Listening?* I turn to inspect but don't see anything unusual. He ignores the noise. "He'd had enough. Seen these stinking Communists from the inside."

Secret talks in Washington, a young son's death, cherry blossoms, stinking Communists—I'm in way deeper than I'd expected. Deep enough that I am uncomfortable. What if someone overhears? The old man leans toward me, puts his hand on my arm again. "When the wall went up, Dieter understood what was happening. He told me we had to get out. I was too old, didn't want to go, but he was desperate for freedom. He made a dash for it. He knew the risk."

An awkward silence dangles in the air, like the sunset fading behind the Brandenburg Gate. "They call it the gate of peace," he mumbles. "More like the gate of Hell."

"I'm so sorry." Instinctively I scan around us.

"Bastards," he says. "I could be shot for saying that, but so what?"

What do you say to a man who's just told you his son was shot while trying to escape from his country? I turn behind us to where I'd heard the sound in the bushes. "I wish—"

"Wishes," he cuts me off. "Wishes are the food of fools. Tell me about the sunset."

Taken aback by the sudden shift of topic. I look out, beyond the Brandenburg Gate, where a last, faint glow of the sunset lingers. "Okay," I say.

"Okay," he breaks into a broad smile. "'Okay,' that's what Dieter used to say. He picked it up from the Americans in Washington. 'Don't use that word in this country,' I told him. 'Okay,' he said. 'I won't use it anymore.' But of course he did."

I want to hug him. Of course, I don't. We talk for a while longer. The sun disappears. The wind picks up. I am required by regulations to be back in West Berlin before nightfall. We stand to say our good-byes, then he heads off down Unter den Linden Strasse. I stand there alone for a few more moments, musing how real connection is possible, even across walls of politics, ideology, and age, beyond good guys and bad guys, but maybe we have to be blind to allow it.

How is it that this old man, who is exactly what I had hoped for and yet so much beyond what I had expected, appeared, just at the moment when I despaired? Almost as if he were sent, something beyond coincidence. I am contemplating this weird turn of…what should I call it?…fate, when I hear a quick tap-tap behind me and turn in time to see my blind friend shuffling back toward me. There is an urgency about him this time. "I don't know your name," he says. "I have to know your name."

"It's Peter."

He smiles. Those teeth again. "Ahhhhh, yes. Peter." He nods. "Of course, Dieter and Peter." He spreads his arms wide, looks into me with his sightless eyes, then wraps me in a huge hug. I smell a faint whiff of sauerkraut on his breath. I've never been hugged by a man before. Never. Not even by my father. Are men supposed to hug? But instinctively I sink into his arms and rest my head on his shoulder. We stand like that for a long time before he pulls back, but still holding me between his outstretched arms.

"Dieter and Peter," he nods. "You could have been friends."

"Could have been friends." I think about that one. The wind gusts and he is gone. I am alone again. I walk slowly back to West Berlin, through the wall.

Chapter 11

Mom's bedroom, on the third floor of Mayma and Grandpa's house, was the only room where I could leave my toys out. I was lying on the floor playing with my Lionel train, the one with real smoke coming out the smoke stack, when I heard the first siren outside. I rushed to the window in time to catch the first ambulance streaking by. Then came the huge hook and ladder, with firemen hanging out the windows, clinging to the poles and this one fireman sitting way up high at the back, steering, followed by more bright and shiny fire engines and the police and the ambulances, and the fire chief, all clanging and banging down Florida Avenue to the Mattress and Box factory. I imagined being a fireman, rushing down the street, just like that, all the traffic halting and everyone watching from their windows, but when I told Mom I was going to be a fireman, she barely looked up from brushing her hair, and when I told her again, she smiled in such a way that I understood I was not going to be a fireman.

"Or maybe a baseball player," I suggested. I'd forgotten all about soccer.

By this time, we'd bought a black-and-white TV so Grandpa could watch the news. The TV was a huge dark box, with a small round screen in the middle, about the size of the round glass window in the door to the washing machine. There were four channels, though the black channel knob had nine numbers on it. At night sometimes we watched baseball, the Washington Senators. Mickey Vernon at first, Eddie Yost at third, Sid Hudson on the mound. The Senators almost always lost, but I didn't understand or care much about the score. I studied Vernon and Yost, how they walked and talked. I wanted to chew gum like them, tap the plate with my big bat like them, pull my visor down low over my eyes and pound my fist into my mitt. If I could learn these things, then I'd be okay, I was sure. People would cheer me when I came out onto the field. The loneliness would go away, and all would be well with the world.

Mayma and Grandpa's house was filled with locked rooms. Locked rooms meant secrets and secrets were there for a boy to explore. The adult world was filled with mystery, secrets hidden behind locked doors, in tiny boxes and old trunks, in black bags, in basements, attics, and bathrooms. It was my job to uncover and explore as many of these secrets as I could, to explore but never to be discovered.

On the fourth floor, near the room where Jock and I slept, was a room that had once belonged to my Uncle Paul, a large man with a small, turned-up nose and a cigarette always drooping from his mouth like a wilted daisy. Uncle Paul stuttered around town in the biggest, dirtiest station wagon in Washington, piled full of fascination. I smashed my nose up against the window and tried to make it all out, boxes filled with broken knobs from old radios; heaps of clear, plastic reels of slick brown recording tape; and batteries—big, round batteries and small, square batteries and long batteries and batteries the size of your thumb; and boxes of wire, tied and rolled, black and silver and copper; and glass tubes and broken pieces of records, and speakers the size of my bed; and clocks and cameras and three calico cats that lived in the boxes that filled the car that trucked around the neighborhood and set me to wondering if Uncle Paul had any inkling about all the bits and pieces of fascination he toted about in his huge car.

The ash on the end of Uncle Paul's cigarette was always within seconds of collapse. It halted conversation, everyone's attention glued, countdown to the inevitable. "Uncle Paul, the ash on your…it's about to…" Uncle Paul droned on and the ashes fell and he swept them away and continued on with his long-winded sentences that no one had been listening to and then he lit another cigarette and the countdown started all over again.

I figured out how to jimmy the lock to Uncle Paul's old room in Mayma and Grandpa's house. I pushed open the door, but the room was so full, the door wouldn't open. When I finally wedged it open enough so I could stick my head in, I was met by another warehouse of old electronics. Nothing worked. It was a boy's dream.

But the most exciting locked room in the house was Grandpa's walk-in closet, which was usually locked but very occasionally, mistakenly left open. Both sides of the closet were lined with shelves. On the left, five hundred boxes of bicycle playing cards, half red and half blue, and on the right, more cartons of Lucky Strikes than one man could smoke in a century. Grandpa planned to spend eternity in a smoke-filled card room.

And then there was Mom's bathroom closet, where her skirts hung all in a row, at my eye level. When I was sure that no one was around, I snuck in, locked the door, and slipped a skirt over my head. Sometimes I took off all my clothes and put on one of her pink girdles, and strutted around in front of the mirror. On the top shelf of Mom's bathroom closet, in a shoebox at the back, I discovered the enema bag with the long nozzle that appeared after Dr. Todd's visits. Dr. Todd, who was brought into this world to torment children. Dr. Todd, who slid into my room, his breath smelling like old cigarettes, the few remaining strands of his black hair greased back like iron spikes. Dr. Open-your-mouth-stick-out-your-tongue-pull-down-your-pants Todd, with his huge hypodermic needle in hand, ready for the stab. He held his needle up to the light and tapped it with his finger. "Hmm," he mumbled as he poked around my bottom, looking for the ideal spot. He poked and prodded and whispered his parting instructions for torture to Mom. After he left, Mom stuck the enema in and pumped me full with warm, soapy water that made me desperate to go. The whole thing was humiliating. And oddly enticing.

I don't think Mom ever suspected that I tried on her clothes, but a woman has a sixth sense about her personal items. If she ever suspected, she never said a word. We were good at secrets.

There were secrets hidden in the walls and under the tongues of the family. We tiptoed around and spoke in whispers and avoided the unmentionables, the interesting things.

On Sundays, we went to St. Matthew's Catholic church on M Street, the site, many years later, of JFK's funeral service. St. Matthew's is a pompous building, designed, it seemed to me, to make children feel small and insignificant. It succeeded in that. Gold-painted vaults above and marble floors below echoed like calls from the dead. The show was run by men dressed in long, funny robes, who turned their backs toward me and droned on in an incomprehensible language. No one ever laughed. They talked about sin and suffering and an angry God who knows even our most secret thoughts. They talked mostly about this thing called death and this place called Hell. Whenever they talked about death, they looked upward, as if what they wanted to say was written on the ceiling. Death, I understood, must be a cross between a ghost and a dragon, something dangerous and frightening.

Mom knelt on the kneelers at St. Matthews and buried her head deep in her hands. When she finished praying, she had red splotches all over her face. She frowned, as if she'd just had a severe talking-to from God himself. After she'd prayed, the wrinkles on her brow burrowed deeper, her shoulders slumped lower. I didn't know whether God wasn't answering calls that day, or perhaps he'd given her some bad news. Something was wrong, I was sure. Maybe it was me.

*

Mr. Poppers lived in the red brick apartment building next door to Mayma and Grandpa's house. He sat for hours in a green canvas lawn chair, on the sidewalk, watching the cars pass by. He nodded at me when I walked by, but we never talked. I looked down on him from my fourth-story window, so what I knew best was his broad-brimmed white straw hat, which he was constantly adjusting, bending the brim this way and that, twirling the hat around on his head. One day, as I was gazing down on the hat from my window, Mr. Poppers jerked violently. The white straw hat slipped off as his head slumped to one side. His left hand dropped to the sidewalk. He jerked once more, like a hiccup this time, and then all was still, his white straw hat lying, brim down, on the ground. I watched for a while, but he didn't move. A while later, Mrs. Poppers came outside and called him. She froze when she saw him all slumped over, picked up a twig from the sidewalk, and poked him in the rib. He didn't respond. She went inside and returned with a sheet, which she tossed over him, then she disappeared again, back inside. A black Cadillac arrived. Two men in dark suits put the sheet and Mr. Poppers on a stretcher, which they slid into the back of the car, then they drove away. The next day, I sat in the living room window, watching. The street was eerily vacant without Mr. Poppers. His white straw hat lay crumpled in the garbage can. When Grandpa poked his head in the room, I asked, "Why did Mr. Poppers throw away his straw hat?"

"We didn't know Mr. Poppers," he said.

"He wore that straw hat every day," I said.

"Mr. Poppers is gone." Grandpa lit a Lucky Strike.

"You mean he's turned into a dragon?" I asked.

"A dragon?" Grandpa shook his head. "You've been reading too many fairy tales. He's not a dragon. He's dead."

Something about this word "dead." Something beyond ghosts and dragons. *When you're dead, all that's left of you is your straw hat in the garbage.* An icy thought rose inside me. *Why don't I ever hear about Dad?* "Is Dad…dead too?" I asked Grandpa.

Grandpa frowned and inhaled his cigarette. When he blew the smoke out, it fogged over the window. "Dead. No…Yes. Well, he might as well be."

Chapter 12

My Air Force tour of duty in Germany is drawing to a close. I contemplate my future and find myself swimming in a sea of doubt. I tell friends I'm going to start the Don Quixote Spoon Co., a fantasy import-export business. It's a joke I've told too often. I know nothing about imports or exports, have not taken one step toward learning, and have not the slightest idea of how I might proceed. The future is whatever shows up. To chart one's life takes confidence in a path. The only path I have confidence in is doubt. I am unable to take my own future seriously.

Norman, my Air Force replacement, and I board a cruise boat for a trip down the Rhine. We join a group of about fifty tourists, stake out a spot on the starboard side, near the bow of the boat, open a bottle of Riesling, lean back to soak up the sun and rock to the gentle bobbing of the Rhine. An attractive woman with short strawberry blonde hair saunters over.

"I heard you speaking English. I'm Sally." Her voice is sultry, low. She presents her hand and holds mine just a smidge longer than I'd expect. She's dressed in a matching olive green blouse and short skirt that exposes enough of two beautiful legs to make me eager to see the rest. She notices my noticing. "You like my Israeli army uniform?"

"You're in the Israeli army?" Mouth before mind again. I hate that I ask the obvious questions.

"Do I look like a soldier?"

I shake my head. "What are you doing in Germany?"

She grabs a cup from a nearby table and holds it out, as if I'm the waiter. Obediently I pour the wine. She winks, then slurps. "I had to get out of town." Brassy as a fire engine, this Sally. Or if she's not the fire engine, maybe she's the fire.

My cue again. "Out of town. Why?"

"Raymond."

"What was wrong with Raymond?"

She places herself on the bench between Norman and me. Her face darkens. "Guys showed up at my house with shotguns, said they were going to shoot his kneecaps off."

"Nice friends you have."

"Had." She brushes the topic off as if it were a crumb that had fallen onto her lap. "I bought a VW camper and an open-ended ticket to Frankfurt. So, here I am."

Norman's eyes narrow to a pinprick. My eyes widen. "Where are you and your camper going?"

"Siegfried."

I scan my mental map of Germany, but nothing registers. "Where's Siegfried?"

"Parked over behind the boat house. Siegfried is my van." She shrugs. "We're going wherever the spirit takes me. I'm alone. Something will show up." Her eyes carom around the boat, then settle on me again. *Is this fire engine real, or is she Hollywood?* We talk and drink, drink and talk. Norman disappears. I don't remember much else from that day, but I do recall a shudder of surprise when I wake up the next morning in a German gasthof. When I turn over, there she is: the fire engine from San Francisco. Over breakfast, I invite her to visit me in Eichenzell, the village east of Frankfurt where I live. Three days later, she moves in. After two weeks, she puts a piece of gray duct tape down the middle of the bed, our private Berlin wall. "You sleep over there," she gestures with an authoritative middle finger. "This is my side." She flashes a coy smile. "But you can come visit."

I return from work one day to discover Sally has rearranged the living room, cleaned out my record collection and trashed the albums she disapproves of.

"Those were my albums," I protest.

"Look at this stuff," Sally flips a few of my records on the floor. "You didn't have any Dylan, so I tossed the Simon and Garfunkel and bought you two Dylan albums. You're going to love *Highway 61 Revisited.*"

"I like Simon and Garfunkel."

"They were okay before they sold out. Don't you worry, Booboo. I'll expand your musical horizons." She's never called me Booboo before. Does this mark a deepening of our relationship? Or are we auditioning for Sesame Street?

We almost break up over the record business, but Sally is in no hurry to leave and I am too mired in doubt to tell her to go. We opt for a mediator. Sally creates a judge's wig, sewing hundreds of cotton balls on a hairnet. We give the wig to Frau Klinke, a sixtyish butterball German hausfrau neighbor, who willingly becomes our official arbiter. This works fine for me because Sally speaks no German and Frau Klinke speaks no English. I translate the proceedings. I win the case, but there's no penalty to the loser. Sally stays on and I stay quiet. Victory is not all its cracked up to be.

Six weeks later, I take a European discharge from the Air Force. We pack Siggy with Sally's miniskirts and my business shirts, her marijuana and my Jameson's Irish Whiskey, her Scrabble game, my maps and books. With no plan as to where we might go, how long we might stay, or what might happen next, we head for the rainbow. I remember what she said on the boat shortly after we met: "Something will show up."

I guess I am what showed up. Sally, Siggy, and I vagabond across Europe, north to south, Ireland to Morocco, east to Romania, and west to Portugal, twelve countries and seven thousand miles in nine months.

We don't kill each other. Which is good, but we travel like astronaut and cosmonaut orbiting together in space— no common language, but sealed by circumstance in the same capsule. How can two people cohabit such tight quarters yet be so far apart? We intuit our direction, one day at a time, stumbling between wild adventures, on a crooked path to nowhere. Much of the time, I don't know where I am or where I'm going, but Sally is never in doubt. Looking back, I wonder what it was that brought us together— other than a long day's drinking into the night. We wanted such different things. Sally wanted to control everything, and thought she had a right to do so. I wanted...what did I want? I had no idea. Maybe I wanted to be controlled. So we were perfectly matched, after all. A follower needs a leader. I was a good little puppy.

We host a party on a collective farm in Romania and trip out on a smuggler's boat off the coast of Yugoslavia.

We smoke the last of our pot two days before border police unbolt Siggy piece by piece as we enter Bulgaria. We spend one entire Christmas day in Siggy, on the side of the Autobahn in Austria, buried in a snowdrift, washing away the jangle of jingle bells with a jug of Irish whiskey.

We've been traveling for nine months when we arrive in Kavala, a Greek fishing town on the North Aegean coast. Kavala is mesmerizing, founded in the seventh century BC, with its own island, Thasos, beckoning from a half-mile off shore. We loll about on white sandy beaches as the hot-tongued Greek sun licks our backs. We snorkel in pristine turquoise water and climb the cobblestone streets, our wicker Yugoslav water jug overflowing with retsina, the cheapest, foulest, most delicious wine anywhere. We watch old men in black berets and white shirts, who look like they've been at the same rickety tables since the time of Alexander the Great. Deep creases like dried riverbeds zag across their necks and faces as they sit, still as statues, frozen in time over their checkerboards. In the warm evenings, Sally and I loll for hours, drinking murky ouzo, nursing the buzz, watching the moon dance across the waves, as hundreds of cats slurp up the fishy remnants from the port streets. We dine on fish that leap from the sea direct to our plates, for the price of a milkshake in the United States.

A week into Kavala, I realize that my chance meeting with Sally has morphed way beyond our improbable one-night stand. While I looked the other way, we became a couple, and now the vagabond thing has become a life-style. We are together because…we are together. She moved in and rearranged my records and never left. It's not bad. Neither is it good. It just is. Sometimes I feel guilty.

Shouldn't I clarify my feelings or intentions toward her? My intentions are hard to clarify because I have none. My guilt is nothing a few glasses of retsina can't disguise.

Sally is always a step or two ahead of me. As we drain another glass or five of retsina, she says, "Let's stay in Kavala for a while?"

"What would we do?" I ask. *And shouldn't I be getting on with my life?*

"Something will show up." *She's like a Greek chorus.* "The Universe provides."

That evening, we join the nightly promenade around the town square, where we meet a tall man with curly blond hair, speaking American English to his young son and fluent Greek to the locals. Sally circles her prey. We're soon drinking with Don and Julie Cummings and their six-year-old son, the only other Americans in Kavala. I listen while Sally shares her fantasy about life in Kavala.

"We've been here for two years," Don says. "Teaching English in the Stratighakis language school. We're returning to the States. If you're interested, you could take over our jobs."

Sally beams. "How perfect. See, Peter, I told you something would show up."

I nod. When destiny knocks you on the head, it's best to bow. After making arrangements to start teaching in the fall, Sally and I depart for more travel. We spend the summer in Ireland, where I scour bookstores to find the one and only Greek language primer in Dublin, a faded hardback that must have languished on a dusty shelf since publication in 1948. Lesson One teaches us the completely useless sentence, "The girl with the beautiful brown eyes was elected queen of the ball." Certain that I'll never have an opportunity to use it, I practice this sentence over and over anyway, working on my accent, getting accustomed to the sounds, living with the rhythm of the language, working until I can speak my one Greek sentence like a native.

Sally and I return to Greece in early September. By this time, "the colonels," a junta of take-no-prisoners thugs, have assumed power. Tanks and soldiers crowd the streets. Shortly after we cross the border, we come to a roadblock, manned by a group of zealous soldiers. They order us out of Siggy. The soldiers demand passports, driver's licenses, health papers, and proof of financial solvency. Disturbed by a picture of a gun on the cover of my James Bond paperback, they confiscate the book. They pummel us with questions. It's all Greek to me, but when I spread my hands in despair and tell them I don't understand, they repeat the questions, ever louder, ever faster, arms gesticulating in ever larger orbits. I point to my ear and shake my head. They wave the spy book in my face, point to the picture of the gun, walk around the car, grab the keys, kick the tires, empty our suitcases, search under the car mats, then return to shout in my face again. They work themselves into a frenzy of xenophobia. They wave their machine guns close enough that I can smell the grease and see the dirt under the nail of the finger that hovers around the trigger. I imagine my body slumped over the steering wheel, bullet holes through my back, blood smeared across the seat. "He died for James Bond" will be inscribed, perhaps in Greek, on my tombstone. If there is a tombstone.

A machine gun barrel pokes my ribs. This is no longer amusing. I clear my throat, and reach back into memory for a "Hail Mary" pass. Lesson one from the 1948 Greek grammar book I studied in Dublin answers my prayer. I spit out my one and only fluent Greek sentence, "The girl with the beautiful brown eyes was elected queen of the ball."

The Earth stands still. The jabbing machine gun drops. The soldiers look at one another, then at us. They repeat my sentence, quietly, looking at one another, then over and over again, louder and louder, then all at once, like a Greek chorus. One of them puts his arm around my shoulder, then spouts an affectionate phrase that sounds like "best friends forever." He tosses the James Bond book back in the car. A young sergeant grabs something from his pack then offers us olives and feta cheese. They open the car door, motion us to get in, hand back the keys, then close the door as if we're royalty. They stand back, salute, and signal us to pass.

And that is how the girl with the beautiful brown eyes became not just queen of the ball, but my Greek Goddess of the Miraculous Rescue.

✱

One week later, I bury all my doubts about Sally and me and the future and hand two hundred Greek drachmas ($35 US) to our landlord, a month's rent for a house on a cobblestoned street, up a hill that leads to a castle, in the old Turkish part of the town. When the roof leaks, we place pots and pans in strategic spots around the house. During one particularly violent storm, a long, mournful howl seeps in through the gap under the front door. On the front steps, we find a huge black-and-white sheepdog, rain soaked and half dead, his bloody left front paw mangled and raw to the bone. His brown eyes are rolled back in his head. "We have to help him," I say.

"What would we do with such a big dog?" Sally asks.

I drop the conversation and bring him inside. His paw is mangled beyond recognition, but his eyes are so soft. I sit on the floor with him all that night, stroking his back, holding his paw. "It's going to be okay. We'll get you fixed up." He rests his head on my leg. I think he understands. By the morning, I am in love. I don't know how to explain it, maybe the wounded love the wounded. I feel my heart opening up, with a creak, like a door that has been closed for so long.

When our Greek neighbors see us with this big dog, they shake their heads. They are practical about these things. "He can't run. He can't herd sheep. What use is he? Get rid of him."

I have no answer, but I know he is here for a reason. Sally and I take him to the local vet, who shakes his head. On the third visit, the vet, grown tired of these crazy Americans with their hopeless dog, says, "There is one place, an animal hospital in Thessaloniki (Salonika). Perhaps they can help."

We make an appointment and drive him the two hours west to the big city. The doctors are dubious. They work on horses and sheep and pigs. "This dog," they say, "he'll never work again."

"Parakalo, ton agapo," (Please, I love him) I say in my pigeon Greek.

"We'll have to amputate his leg. It's the only way."

I cringe. They nod, and two weeks later we have a three-legged dog. We name him Tría Pódia, Three Legs, then quickly nickname him Tripod. Tripod soon becomes the love of my life and the most famous dog in Kavala.

Every night at ten o'clock, we sit on the couch together. Tripod takes up most of it. I sit on the end. Tripod rests his head in my lap. I ask him about his day, and he asks me about mine. I rub his soft fur and think about my warped life. Tripod and I are wounded animals, together. "What's to become of us?" I ask him. "You have three legs, and I have a stunted heart." He looks up at me with his brown saucer eyes, and I feel a love the likes of which I haven't felt in a long time, if ever. We have a thing going, Tripod and I. I recognize that it's a bit over the top, maybe way over the top. A psychologist would have a field day with me, but it feels so good to feel what I feel, so I go with it. "It'll all work out," Tripod tells me. He has more faith than I do. We share a cookie, then go to bed.

Teaching and living in Kavala is a magical year, a fairy-tale life, but as school comes to a close, Sally and I both recognize that it's time to go home. Aggregating my Air Force duty, plus my travel, and our teaching time in Greece, I've been away from the United States for almost five years. Time for me to face the Big Book of the Future that I've kept buried for so long.

The hardest part of leaving Kavala is what to do with Tripod. We can't take him with us. We ask everyone we know in Kavala, "Will you take Tripod?" No Greek wants a large three-legged dog. As our time draws to a close, the future does not look good for Tripod. Our search grows more desperate. Then three days before our departure, we find a farmer who agrees to adopt him. The farmer arrives at our house, loads and ties Tripod in the bed of his pickup.

I watch Tripod's mournful, trusting eyes disappear around the bend in the road: How could you? When I can no longer see him, I droop back inside. His big eyes follow me everywhere. I mope around the house, silent, somber, and alone. I sit for an hour on the couch, on the end where I always sat, and run my hand across where Tripod always sat. I break a cookie in half and eat my half. I lay his half on the pillow, in case. I can almost imagine. Wishful fantasy. Tripod is gone. My love has gone.

I think back to my time in Peru and how Violetta dressed in her black mourning clothes. I understand it now. I feel the same. There's no joy in Kavala. We go through the motions, packing up and closing down, getting ready to depart. After dinner we hear a scratch at the front door. A flutter passes through my heart, as if…but of course not. I look at Sally. She shrugs. Should we even investigate? It's the wind, or a stray cat. Kavala, a fishing port, is filled with feral cats. Slowly, I rise and shamble over to the front door and open it. Tripod jumps into my arms. Down we go, rolling together like puppies, laughing and kicking and licking, my arms around his neck, his tail wagging madly, my cries of joy ringing out, tears streaming down my cheeks. Life has meaning again. When we come up for air, he looks at me, his big brown eyes asking the one and only, right question: Now isn't this better?

How he found his way, fifteen miles on three legs, over a route he had travelled just once, tied up in the back of a pick-up, is a mystery I will never understand, part of the magic that happens between man and dog when the heart is open.

With no alternative, we call the farmer. He returns. Tripod is tied and carted away again.

My heart breaks. I wake up that night with the disturbing realization: I am bonded to this dog deeper than I ever will be to Sally. What kind of a man am I? Can I even love another human? Or am I a tin man with no heart?

I shove such questions as far back as I can and say nothing to Sally. I don't have language for it, and lack the courage to try, except through clumsy, unspoken withdrawal.

"You're going to love San Francisco," Sally says. "Once we're settled, we'll plan the future." Whose future is she talking about? Why am I going to San Francisco? What is this relationship all about? I don't want to return to Washington, so following Sally out to California is an easy path. But it feels like I'm lugging around a sack of stones that I can't put down: feelings and decisions and procrastinations and guilt. Something is way off, and I think it's me.

We depart Kavala and drive Siggy through the winding roads of the French Riviera, along the Costa Brava and Costa del Sol in Spain, to Lisbon, Portugal, where Sally and I settle in for a two-week stay while we await Siggy's passage back to the United States. The day we arrive, the talk is all about a meningitis scare in the pool. Two days later, it's confirmed. Two children are hospitalized in critical condition. The pool is drained and closed. Foreboding settles over the campers.

I pace about, read, take desultory walks around Lisbon. I'm eager to get back to the States, ready for something, though I have no idea what that something should be. My thoughts bounce back constantly to Tripod. I see a dog running at the campsite. I think of Tripod. I see a rope hanging on a fence. I'm reminded of his leash by our front door. Why this ill-fated obsession? He was a wonderful dog, but he was an interlude. We had him for six months only. I wanted so badly to bring him back to the States, but it was impossible. So why does he haunt me still? Slowly the reality sinks in. I've been in Europe five years. I've experienced a lot and learned a lot during this time. But nothing more important than what I learned from Tripod: what it's like to love and be loved.

Chapter 13

I was nine, wobbling on the edge of innocence. Dad was gone, as usual. I spent my summer days wandering around my grandparents' big country house in the Blue Ridge Mountains of Pennsylvania, searching for something to do that would register five to six on the scary scale, but still this side of terrifying.

At night, Mom, my sister Virginia, and I sat on the porch, in the white wicker chairs, drinking lemonade through colored straws, falling asleep as Grandpa grumbled on about distant relatives, aching knees, and old age, not my idea of adventure.

Before going to bed, I set five dog biscuits on the bottom step of the front porch, for Cedar, the neighborhood collie mutt. Cedar was my best friend. I'd saved up my weekly twenty-five-cents allowance for a whole month and bought Cedar a box of Milk-Bone dog biscuits. Chicken and beef, his favorite.

The next morning, I was the first one awake. I rushed downstairs, out to the porch where Cedar was waiting for me, just as I'd hoped he would be, thumping his tail on the wet grass. I scratched his silky ears. He licked my arm and snuggled against me, resting his chin on my foot and cocking his head to one side.

That's when I noticed it, there on the porch step, the box of dog biscuits, empty, ripped open, box destroyed, not a crumb left. I realized right away. I'd left the box outside all night. Biscuits gone, my month's allowance gone, the fun of putting out biscuits every night gone, Cedar waiting for me each morning, over. All of it over. I wanted to grab and shake Cedar, but you can't scold a puppy for eating dog biscuits. Cedar wagged his tail, and all I could do was hug him.

✱

When you're nine, everything is big and bold, and anything is possible. The night before the fireman's carnival, I fantasized for hours about riding the Ferris wheel. From the top of the Ferris wheel, I could reach out and touch a star, and when I touched a star, surely that would end the loneliness. I had no idea that a force beyond my imagination was about to ambush me, zap me up to Heaven, flip me like a cosmic pizza, then topple me off the wall of childhood, split into more pieces than Humpty Dumpty.

On the way to the fairgrounds, I asked Mom, "Can I ride the Ferris wheel this year, please?"

"We'll see."

"That's what you said last year."

As soon as we parked the car, I pressed Mom again. "Please, Mom, huh?"

"You're too little," Virginia said. Two inches taller than me, she was just a girl, afraid of Ferris wheels too.

At the fairground, bright lights and streams of flags stoked my dreams. The smell of cotton candy mixed with the hawkers' call, "Hey, step right up here, easy, easy, take home a teddy bear for the lady." We walked down game booth alley—ring toss, cork guns, cover the spot, roller-ball, jugglers, and acrobats, across from tents and tractors, a kaleidoscope of color and action. Then there were the rides: the Zipper, Scooters, Monkey Maze, the pony rides. Teenage boys strutted about, arms skating around their girls' waists. The boys stopped to toss baseballs at bowling pins, as the girls shifted nervously from foot to foot, twirling a curl to the voice of Bobby Womack: "If you think you're lonely now."

And rising like a queen in the middle of the world, higher than anything, more elegant, more exciting than every ride and game and flag put together, beckoning me with red, white, and blue flashing lights: the Ferris wheel. I watched her circle, off to Heaven with her lucky passengers, up and away.

The new moon rose. The jokester dangled his feet. I tugged at Mom's skirt. My eyes begged shamelessly. I watched the wheel circle around and around…around and around and around, until I was dizzy with watching. "Please!"

Mom looked at me, then she looked at the Ferris wheel. I watched a girl with a blonde ponytail standing by the Ferris wheel, then I nudged closer to Mom and tugged her hand. "Well…okay," she said, but she wasn't finished. "If…" It seemed like she was waiting for the sun to rise. "If you find someone to accompany you."

"You come."

She shook her head. "I don't like heights."

I looked toward Virginia. No way. I scanned the crowd for someone I knew, anyone. I looked left, right. No one. Then I spotted her again, the blonde ponytail, still there, swaying gently, bobbing as she watched the Ferris wheel turn. She raised her right hand and pointed, as if beckoning me. The moon swallowed my shyness. I pulled my hand away from Mom and dashed over to ponytail. "I want to go on the Ferris wheel, but my mom says I have to go with someone. Will you?"

"You want me to ride the Ferris wheel with you?" Her lips curled. A slow smile spread. For a moment I thought maybe she was laughing at me. "Sure," she says. "That would be fun."

I waive to Mom, and she nods back, casual, as if this is something that happens every day.

Ponytail looks at me as we join the line. "My name is Emily." She is somewhere between fifteen and fifty.

"Do you like Ferris wheels?" I ask.

She nods.

"I do, a lot," I tell her, and then we're silent, shuffling up to the front of the line. A burly operator in a muscle-man T-shirt, a dragon tattooed on his arm, spits his chewing tobacco as we present our tickets. He grabs my shoulder. "Hang on, kid. How old are you, six?"

"I'm nine. I'll be ten in—"

"Well, you're a little squirt. Move over here." He directs me to the measuring post.

"I'm with *her*." I point to Emily.

Dragon Man looks Emily up and down and snickers. "Startin' pretty young, ain't ya?"

"I'm fifteen," she says.

"Mom said I could go with her," I say.

"Don't matter none to me what ya mom says. If you ain't big enough, you don't ride."

I look toward Mom, but she's watching the Zipper. Dragon Man grabs the brake to the Ferris wheel and tugs it hard. I'm usually shy with adults, but now I'm filled with a rush of energy I've never known before. "You get to run the Ferris wheel all by yourself? That's so cool."

Dragon Man looks at Emily again and flexes his arm, and I swear, the dragon in his tattoo smiles at me. "Your lucky day, kid. You're right on the line. Get in." He raises the bar, motions us to sit. I climb in. Emily follows. Dragon man tosses a brown wool blanket over our laps, then locks the bar.

The motor purrs, and the Ferris wheel jerks backward. We stop, then another lurch, forward this time, and we're off. I grip the bar with both hands. My tummy does a somersault. When we reach the top, my legs tingle. Emily and I, tucked under one blanket, our legs touching as we start to descend, hips rocking together now, sliding back and forth, turning to look briefly at each other, smiling, picking up speed, climbing again, leaving Earth behind, even as my arm is in pins and needles and pressed against the arm rest, but I dare not move, dare not disturb anything, a small pock mark on her forehead, just above her left eye, where I could reach over and touch it if I dared, which I don't, and then she laughs aloud, I don't know why but it doesn't matter, she laughs with her red lips spread apart in the black night so I can see her teeth, and I feel her bare arm against mine, and our legs touching, like a tiny kiss under the blanket, as she tosses her head back and her ponytail brushes against my neck, as we swing forward and back and forward, and I want to rock the seat and feel her hair again, and then she laughs and I laugh and we rock as we climb again and again, and the moon smiles and the people below are tiny specks and a shiver shoots down my spine, and then I am gone, gone as my heart tumbles and my head floats, over and above and beyond the clouds, and higher and higher, and I do actually touch a star, up and away and gone, gone! everlasting, splashing, smashing, totally gone, wow, whoopee, zingo, GONE! Time lost. And then, we descend, slowly, slowly, back, back down to Earth, down to the end, down to stop, down. Dragon Man lifts the bar. He grabs the blanket. Emily jumps out. "Thanks," she says, and I watch her ponytail disappear into the crowd.

"Ride's over, Sonny. Time to get out."

I lift myself off the seat and down, leaving the Ferris wheel, stumbling through the crowd, over to where Mom stands, watching the Zipper. "How was that?" she asks, but I don't answer. She wouldn't understand. No one could understand what happened up there. I don't even understand. I want to tell the whole world, but I don't tell anyone because no one could understand. No one has ever felt how I felt.

Well, I do tell Cedar. When we get home, I sit on the bottom porch step next to Cedar and tell him all about it. He wags his tail.

The next day, I woke up thinking about Emily, about how our hips had rubbed together under the blanket and the beautiful mark above her left eye. I ran to the phone to call her. We had one of those party lines; everything had to go through the operator. As soon as the operator answered, I said, "I want to talk to Emily."

"Emily…who?"

"Emily. You know, from the carnival, the Ferris wheel."

The laugh on the other end was not even halfway funny. "I weren't at the Ferris wheel, son. You tell me Emily's daddy's name, and I'll connect you." Then the line went dead.

I asked Mom to help me find Emily's phone number.

"Where does she live?"

"I don't know."

"You don't know her name. You don't know where she lives. I'd like to help, but you're not going to find that girl." I knew Mom couldn't understand. I spent the next three hours calling every "E" in the phone book. "Is your name Emily? Were you at the fireman's carnival yesterday? Did we ride the Ferris wheel together?"

"No, not me."

"No, I didn't go the carnival."

"No, I don't like Ferris wheels."

I talked to half the county, but never to Emily.

That night, I lay in bed for a long time thinking. Thinking about the Ferris wheel, about loneliness, most of all, about Emily. Thinking about the little mark over her left eye, remembering Emily's leg rubbing against mine. Remembering the brush of her ponytail on my neck and the tickle that showed up somewhere deep inside me. Wondering if anyone else had ever felt that same tickle. Wondering if Emily had felt it. Emily.

Chapter 14

Sally gets me to San Francisco. Six weeks later, we break up. "Good-bye, Booboo," she says. And it's over.

I meet Jennifer on a ski weekend at Lake Tahoe and slide into a new relationship. Jennifer is soft and smooth in all the ways that Sally was hard and angular.

"So what's this workshop all about?" I ask Jennifer as we drive north on I-5 from San Francisco to Ashland, Oregon, for what she describes as a "workshop with the great Carl Rogers." We cross the Siskiyou Summit, catching our first view of the Rogue River Valley, ringed by mountains, ridges beyond ridges, receding as far as we can see, green to blue-green, to blue, to gray. I roll down the windows to breathe in the sweet pine smells of the mountain air. "I hope this won't be some touchy-feely, woo-woo thingy."

"A little woo-woo wouldn't hurt you." Jennifer gives me a lemon look. We're at a delicate point in our relationship, which has lurched from delicate point to delicate point for its entire six-month life. Sally and I were willing to hide behind curtains, but Jennifer pulls back the curtains and leaves us standing awkward and naked. What's the joy of that?

It's 1974. I'm thirty-two. I've been living on the West

Coast for nine months, but I'm still disoriented. To a long-time East Coaster, the ocean is stubbornly on the wrong side. I'm in a new home now, with a new job, and a new girlfriend. Everything new but the same old me. Same old doubts. "You said this workshop is to be run by Carl somebody," I ask Jennifer as we descend into the Rogue Valley. "Who is he, anyway?"

"Carl Rogers, the father of humanistic psychology."

"I should be impressed?"

Jennifer gives me the look. I pretend not to see.

We drive about, exploring a few side roads on the way to Ashland. Weatherworn, lichen-covered fences nestle into the rolling hills. In the meadows, huge boulders lie abandoned like some ancient giant's now unwanted marbles. Similar boulders line both sides of long dirt drive-ways that disappear into the pines. Man seems to cohabit easily with nature here. We pull into town. Ashland smiles: Elizabethan banners, flowers, flags, bright-colored clothes, young couples kissing on corners, elderly couples holding hands while watching young couples kissing, faces glowing. Drugs? I wonder. Mysticism? Voodoo? Woo-woo? How can a town be this happy? What's the catch?

A plaza at the center of town bursts with life. A group of scantily clad, seldom-washed long hairs strum guitars, beat tambourines, and sing off key. Tangled up among the five of them are four small dogs and six backpacks. A sign leaning against an open guitar case says, "Please don't feed the hippies."

Jennifer and I claim a spot in a camping site north of town, set up our tent, and roll out our double mattress. Jennifer distributes her homemaking toys—candles, incense, music. I crawl into bed with a book. Most of the workshop participants are housed on the university campus, but I'm happy to be camping away from the crowd. I need my private cave, a place for escape in case this whole workshop churns up more woo-woo than I can do-do.

I'm not a group person, but the next morning, promptly at nine as instructed, we join the group: 120 of us, mostly in our twenties or thirties, gathered in a large wood-paneled room on the campus of Southern Oregon College (now University). Jennifer places herself near the front row, center. I find a spot in the back row, where we wait for the workshop to begin. We sit, watching the wall clock stutter forward. Five past nine, ten past, quarter past. Shouldn't the Father of Humanistic Psychology be a bit more on time than this?

I wonder what Jennifer is thinking. We haven't even started, and already the weirdness is seeping in. Finally, a girl in short cut-offs stands. "What's the story here? It's twenty minutes after the scheduled start, and nothing is happening."

As the grumbles grow, a woman with short blonde hair, midthirties, stands. "Actually a lot is happening. You are all here because you made a choice to be here. Same for me." Her voice is calm and confident. "We've been sitting, all of us, together, more or less compliantly, then this lady…what's your name? Cat, thanks…Cat stood up and spoke her mind." The blonde strides across the front of the room, stops and scans the room. She looks at Cat. "What would you like to see happen?"

"Let's get this workshop started. I came a long way, and—"

"The workshop started twenty minutes ago when you came in. Now you've taken the first step toward assuming responsibility for your time."

"Are you the leader? Why are you playing this game with us?"

"My name is Marian," the blonde says, "and we're playing the game of life together, right here, right now, you and I and all of us."

Cat snorts. "Cut the psycho-bullshit. Please. I paid good money for this. Do you have something to teach us, or are we going to play word games for five days?"

"You sound frustrated. That's energy. Maybe you're a leader here too. Maybe you can help shape our time. Like every moment of your life, this is your moment."

Pockets of grumbling break out across the room, but Marian holds firm. So different from me. I'd have caved in, my doubts directing me to the nearest hideout. Reality sinks in. There is no agenda, but we are free to create one. Or not. There aren't any leaders. Or we are all leaders. The workshop will start at nine. Or whenever we start it. Nothing is certain. Everything is up in the air. Remarkably like life.

It no longer smells like woo-woo, but neither is it hamburger and fries. My stomach rattles with little pebbles, tossed around like they're in a cement mixer. I'm in the perfect incubator for my doubts to flourish.

A woman with soft brown shoulder-length hair speaks up. "My name is Shelah. My husband left me. After eight years." Fissures split her voice in half. "We have a five-year-old daughter." She makes no attempt to hide her grief. "I am so alone. If anyone can help . . ." She dissolves into tears and sits down. Her speech reminds me briefly of my own broken existence. Then my mind switches channels. The chairs are hard. The room is claustrophobic, and I wonder if we're over maximum capacity. I look again for exits: two, three. Is that enough?

Marian takes the floor again. "I feel the transformational potential in the room. The staff will be a resource for you, but you have to do the work. Don't leave here without getting what you came for." She scans the room. A few heads are nodding. Mine is spinning. I want to get outside, into the sunshine. "We expect everyone for a community meeting here, every morning from nine o'clock to eleven o'clock. Otherwise, you are free to do whatever you want. You made a choice to be here. Now make a choice for your life. Be where you need to be and who you need to be, and you will grow, maybe in ways you can't now imagine. The only other scheduled event is that Carl has agreed to demonstrate his approach to psychotherapy. He'll need a volunteer from the group. If you're interested, please speak to him. He's in the back corner."

I notice an elderly man—calm, balding, ordinary looking, no pipe, no monocle, no Sigmund Freud beard—seated in the back. He doesn't stand. He hasn't said a word. I think he's the Father of Humanistic Psychology.

People make suggestions for groups they'd like to form. I don't suggest. The whole thing seems chaotic and disorganized, the perfect breeding ground for doubt. I'm not sure it was a good decision to come. But after lunch, I join a group focused on relationships. Jennifer heads off to Creative Actualizations, whatever that is. Someone in the relationship group—I'm still not sure who are staff and who are participants—suggests that we each start by talking about our current relationship, or lack of one. I'm last to speak. "Jennifer, my girlfriend, tells me she wants more from our relationship. More of what, I don't know. Our relationship...well, it's not really a relationship. It's actually a lot like the last relationship I was in, which wasn't a real relationship either."

Silence greets my remark. *Why do I say such stupid things?* Then the guy who'd begun the topic—maybe he's part of the staff so he's obliged to say something—says, "Forget what *she* wants for a minute. What do you want in a relationship?" I try to think of an answer. Invention fails me. Sure everyone is waiting for my response, I'm self-conscious. "I want what everyone wants, I guess. You know—"

He cuts me off. "I don't know, and I'm not sure you know. If you don't know what you want, you're never going to find it." I keep my mouth shut after that piece of wisdom. For two days, I listen. On sloping lawns and at coffee tables, I witness gatherings of three, four, five, ten people, talking earnestly, listening as if they're trying to hear the sound of cells replicating, reaching out, touching one another, smiling, questioning, crying, struggling, and hugging. Lots of hugging. What is it about hugging? Like some secret handshake? A code? Is everyone speaking some secret language? Am I'm the only one who doesn't speak it? I want to be part of it. I don't want to have anything to do with it. I want. I don't want. I have no idea what I want. Except to get out of doubt.

I'm silent at community meeting, as others spill their innermost traumas. They might as well strip naked. When

I think of speaking myself, my mouth goes dry. Later, back in our tent, Jennifer and I flop down on our mattress. She lights a candle. We've barely seen each other all week. We're silent for a while, watching the flickers dance on the tent wall. "This workshop is so great," she says. "I'm growing so much, so exciting. How is it for you?"

"I'm such a chickenshit."

"That's a new one." She sits up in bed, rests on her elbow. "I haven't heard you say that before."

"I say it all the time, just not out loud."

"How are you a chickenshit?"

"I just am. I don't know. I can't talk about it now." I flop over, try to sleep, but my mind is in dungarees, dressed for digging. I think about Jennifer's question. How am I a chickenshit? These psychologists, they talk about everything, even sex. "Ask for what you want in sex," they say.

The next day, after the morning community meeting, Susan, a spunky psychologist with a head of short, spiked hair like a cute hedgehog, tries to draw me out. "So, Peter, how's the workshop now? Are you making progress?"

"When I came to the workshop, I was lost, but able mostly to hide it from myself. I'm still lost, but now I obsess about it. Is that progress?"

Susan stares into me. "I don't know. How do you feel about it?"

"I feel that I'm spinning around, going nowhere. I'm—"

"The word 'that' introduces a thought." Susan slips her glasses down her nose. "How do you feel?"

"I'd like to have a little—"

"No. Feelings. How do you feel?" she interrupts again. *Is she toying with me?* "You know—angry, frustrated, confused.

Those are feelings." She punctuates her little lesson with a wink. "In case you didn't know."

"I'll take confused for fifty dollars." She doesn't laugh. I go on. "I think I'm—"

"Stay with the feeling. Tell me about 'confused.' Where does it live in your body?"

Others join us and the conversation swerves, but in bed that night, I keep seeing Susan and hearing her voice, "Stay with the feeling." *What does she mean? Psychologists descend from another planet.*

Midweek, Carl gives a demonstration of his approach to psychotherapy. He hasn't said a word in the full group. How's that for the father of humanistic psychology? I almost don't go to the demo, but curiosity gets the better of me. We gather in a large auditorium to watch the great man at work. I find a seat in the front row. Carl and Shelah sit on an otherwise empty stage. I recognize Shelah as one who'd spoken at the community meeting on day one. She slouches low in her chair, fidgeting with her hair. Carl sits across from her, in casual slacks and shirt, bent slightly toward her, like a favorite uncle. Shelah is barely audible. "I don't know where to start."

"It's hard to begin," Carl says. "Is there anything you'd like to tell me?"

"My husband left me two months ago. I wonder if I'll ever smile again." It sounds like hyperbole, but I've noticed how she walks around with her soul at half-mast.

"You miss him a lot," Carl says. "The joy has emptied out of your life."

Shelah lowers her eyes. "I don't care much whether I live or die. Except for Cara, my daughter. She's the only one I care about."

"You care a lot about your daughter, not much about yourself."

I study this Carl guy. *If he's such a hotshot psychologist, why doesn't he tell her what to do?* Instead, he reflects what he hears, the words and the person behind the words—her feelings, her fears and judgments. Shelah begins to open, like a flower. It's as if I'm hearing her soul speak. Their conversation is two people in a crucible of crystal honesty. When there is nothing to say, the silence plays out like a sleepless night. Carl listens to what is not being said as much as to what is being said. He listens to the story behind the story, and somehow, magically, he opens the doors of hope.

Something in me cracks. I drift from the conversation on stage to thinking about how I camouflage my feelings, how I've always thought of feelings as second-rate thoughts, signs of weakness, irritants that will pass and are best ignored until they do. I consider Susan's advice, "Stay with the feeling." What's the cost for ignoring my feelings? When I tune back in, Shelah is sitting up. Her voice smiles.

The day after Carl's demonstration, I stand up at the community meeting for the first time. My mind is rumbling. I have to speak, even with no idea what I want to say. "I feel so lost. Like I don't know who I am, except that I'm filled by doubt, all the time. I pretend I know what I'm doing, but I don't. I'm scared people will see through me, recognize me for the fraud I am." Embarrassment rips off my clothes. I am exposed in front of everyone, just what I had feared most, making a fool of myself. Again. I babble on, certain that Jennifer is laughing at me. "I can't keep living like this. I exist, but nothing more." My teeth chatter; my legs are noodles. "I'm so embarrassed. I'm sorry. I'm so sorry. I shouldn't have . . . I don't even know how to ask for help."

I slump down. Another guy, about my age, in a San Francisco Giants baseball cap, stands up. "I hear an eloquent cry for help. I could have said the same words. That is, I wish I'd said them. Maybe we should form a group of lost boys." His line sparks a ripple of laughter across the room. "And girls," someone adds.

A seed is born, tiny as the beginning of all life, microscopic but determined. We form a small group that we call "The Doubters' Club." For the first time ever, I speak openly about my doubts and fears. A girl in the group tells me I sound "depressed." It's the first time I've ever heard the term. I don't pay it much attention. Someone else labels me "King of Doubt." I feel a speck of pride in the title. Not much to boast about, but it's a start. I think of Brownie, the chestnut I planted twenty-six years ago in Scotland, and imagine a tree now spreading its wings, loaded with chestnuts.

The group staggers through anger, chaos, tentative steps forward and back. Tears, frequent laughter, and the room smells of sex. Everyone in the workshop has read, memorized, and is practicing *The Joy of Sex*. I'm still stuck back in the shame of sex. Liaisons sprout, blossom, and wither in hours or days. Jennifer and I are camping together, but it's unclear if we are a couple or not. I hang out with Susan again. She talks me into cutting class for some skinny-dipping at a local nudie beach on the river. After swimming, I lie in the sun as Susan drips lotion down my spine. She rubs it in, across my back, my buttocks, down my legs.

She dribbles some between my legs, then reaches in to slop it around. I want to turn over, but, well, it's out of the question. Even a nude beach has certain boundaries. I don't tell Jennifer about any of this, but when I get back, I sense Susan's presence between us. Jennifer and I snap at each other. The confusion in our relationship lurks like a terrorist, striking unpredictably and at will.

Something unusual is happening. I have lived for so long in the world of the other that I barely recognize what is inside me. I know only the Demons of Doubt, which drown out all other voices. In Ashland, for the first time, I allow myself into the world of the heart, and I imagine life beyond doubt. I might be able to take charge of my own life, assert myself, listen to my own voice, be me instead of looking over my shoulder to see who was watching and judging. I feel a life within.

I begin to see why they call Carl Rogers the Father of Humanistic Psychology.

With only two days remaining, I return to the campsite. Jennifer stays at the college for an evening meeting of her Creative Actualizations group. She'll return later.

Walking across the campsite to our tent, I stop to listen to the crickets. Their cheery symphony reminds me of what I can now imagine as possibile, but also how far I have still to go. In the tent, I undress slowly, my mind tossing around everything I've been exposed to throughout the week. *Am I missing the boat? Looking for love in all the wrong places? Am I living a life in gray monotones, when a Technicolor world waits around the corner. Do I dare ask? How do you ask?* I've learned some meditation techniques in the workshop, and

I'm eager to use them to quiet my mind so I can listen, as Marian says, to the tiny, wise voice inside. "Quiet the mind enough, and you'll hear the wisdom of your soul."

It's dark in the tent. I light an aroma candle of Jennifer's, breathe in the sweet smell of honeysuckle, and watch the flame flicker. I turn on the tape player. The tent is filled with romantic piano music: "All of Me," "Temptation," "Love Me Tender." In my pajamas now, I sit cross-legged on the double air mattress that is our bed. I close my eyes, focus on my breath. I decide to meditate. In. Out. In. My shoulders relax. Some of the tension subsides, like I'm slipping into a warm bath. Images of Susan and me skinny-dipping at the river invade. Us on the beach, as she dribbles the lotion between my legs. The delight that ran through me as she reached in between my legs to scoop it up. *Wait!, I'm supposed to be meditating, not fantasizing about sex on the beach.* I force myself to focus on my breath again, take myself to a peaceful valley, surrounded by light. I feel the warm sun on my back. I am calm, relaxed, easy. Ah.

"Peter. "

I know the voice. Not Jennifer. But who?

"It's Susan. Can I come in?"

"Susan, I'm…Of course, come in." When I open my eyes, Susan is already inside the tent, dressed in a light pink one piece, so short it might even be a nightdress. Her breasts, soft as silk, poke at my eyes.

"I wanted to see how you were doing? You seemed in such pain earlier."

"I was meditating." Susan looks different in the candlelight, smaller.

"I don't want to interrupt." She turns toward the door.

"I was just…remembering our time at the beach."

Susan tugs her dress. "Well, I should be going."

"Jennifer has a meeting tonight. Sit, stay a while, can you?" She looks around the tent.

"Sit here, on the mattress with me." An invitation. A mistake.

She sits. Whose hand moves first? Does it matter? Hers rests on my thigh. Mine on her back, gently caressing the lovely curve. The music is soft and soothing. "I'm cold," she says. "Can I get under the blanket?"

I pull down the blanket. She crawls under. I slip in next to her. The candle flickers and out. Our legs vine together. The first kiss is tender and soft. *Stop now, or there will be no stopping.* My mind whirls: *what about Jennifer? We haven't promised monogamy, but it's understood. Susan is so cute. What would Jennifer say? Maybe she'd be okay with it. Are you serious? She won't know. I shove my doubts to the background. So much talk this week about living in the moment. It's time to try it.*

After a long, wet kiss, Susan props herself up on her elbow. "So what do you like?"

No one has ever asked me such a question. I have no idea what to say.

"You know," she continues, "in bed, what do you most like to do? Like, I love to go down on a guy. Do you like that?"

What she's suggesting is wild enough, but to talk about it first! If Mom knew about this, she'd—and what is my mother doing here in bed with me and Susan? While I'm still wrapped up in my Oedipal thoughts, Susan disappears under the blankets. She kisses me first on the chest.

My heart beats like a bass drum. She slips off my pajama bottoms. Her hands glide with long, sensuous strokes, up one leg and down the other, then a short stop in the middle. "Ding dong." I close my eyes, habit, I guess, then soar over the rainbow, as I surrender to dreams that bubble up from the underworld of pagan passions, dreams of pleasures not meant for a nice boy from Washington, DC.

How long is Susan under there? A minute, half an hour? I am lost in a world of ecstasy when I hear a muffled voice, "Peter. Are you still awake?"

"Don't stop. Please, don't stop now."

"Don't stop what? You must be dreaming. I'm home." I feel a hand, Jennifer's hand—I'd know that hand anywhere —on my shoulder. *Is this a nightmare? Did I fall asleep? Impossible. No, It's worse than the worst nightmare.* Jennifer scrabbles around the tent searching for matches, then relights the candle. "What an evening, the best discussion I've been in all week. What have you been up to?"

"Up to?" *Is she being funny?* "Me. Ah...nothing much."

"I'm high as can be." Jennifer stoops, about to flop down on the air mattress. She pauses without sitting, looks at me for the first time through the candlelight. She frowns. "Peter, what are you doing under there? Did I interrupt something? You don't have to..."

Under the blankets, Susan backs off her mission for long enough to ask, "What's going on up there? You okay?"

Jennifer bends low over the bed. "Who is that?"

I improvise, fast but not well. "I...uh, hi. I guess I was asleep. Give me a couple of minutes to wake up. Why don't you go wash and brush your teeth? I'll be awake when you come back."

Jennifer stares at me, pale and boot faced. "Who's there?" She rips off the blankets. Susan's backside flaps in the breeze. She doesn't miss a beat. "I was just leaving."

Jennifer is her equal. "Yeah, well you're a few minutes late."

Susan jumps out of bed, looks around for her clothes, but Jennifer is one step ahead of her. She grabs Susan's dress. "Get out."

Susan holds out her hand for her dress. "I don't think so." Jennifer takes the dress over to the candle. I watch the flame grow before she tosses Susan's dress out the door. "You won't be wearing this again."

Chapter 15

Transplanted again, that's how I remember 1952. Back again to England, no more baseball. Cricket was now the game. I dressed in white shirts and shorts and carried around a bat that was three times as wide as a baseball bat. I didn't understand much about the game, but I liked wearing all white, and I loved the chance to play with the smell of freshly mown grass underfoot. We were back with Dad. His smile lit up Dunbritton, our brick house in Shenfield, Essex, a small town about thirty miles northeast of London. Mom had me wear an "I like Ike" badge to school. I didn't know who Ike was or why I liked him, but I wore the badge proudly. When the lads at school asked me about Ike, I told them he was our king. That worked.

Dunbritton was on a double lot, with a spreading lawn, perfect for cricket, but the other boys were more experienced at cricket than me. They had no interest in coming over. I asked Mom to practice with me.

"I don't play cricket," she said.

"It's easy," I scoffed. "Here's the bat. I'll pitch the ball"—technically it was called bowling—"and you hit it."

"What if I miss?" Mom rested the bat on her shoulder like a baseball bat. "It won't hurt me?" She furrowed her brow.

I shook my head.

"You promise?"

I tossed the ball. Mom swung and missed. On my second toss, she missed again, but the ball hit her leg. She clutched the spot, then hopped around whimpering. I didn't believe she was in real pain, but she threw the bat down and ran into the house. "I'm going to soak in a warm bath," she said as she disappeared inside.

I followed close behind, unsure what I'd done, sure that whatever it was, was wrong. There are two kinds of people in this world: those who blame themselves for everything and those who blame themselves for nothing. I was clearly the former.

At dinner, Mom carefully pulled her skirt up a few inches, revealing a bruise on her shin, round and splotchy, the size of a grapefruit, the color of a fig. We spent the whole dinner talking about it. After we'd fallen all over ourselves with sympathy, Mom sat upright. Her eyes pierced. "You have to be more careful."

"I thought—"

"Don't you see what you did? Women are gentle, not rough like boys. You must treat women more delicately." She looked over at Dad. "Otie, you're the man. You should tell him."

Dad squirmed and lit his pipe. It went out. He lit it again. Mom held her fork in the air. Virginia chewed her Yorkshire pudding. I asked to be excused.

"Not yet," Mom said. "Your father wants to talk to you."

Dad drew deep on his pipe and looked out the window.

"Tell him, Otie." Mom propped her elbows on the table.

Dad smiled, whistled a tune. Mom swirled her tongue. Then she rose and departed without another word. The bruise healed, but I can still see it, round and mean, and when it is quiet enough, I hear her voice—or is it now my voice?—"You must treat women more delicately."

✱

At Christmastime, two big packages called from under the tree. Virginia and I picked them up, turned them over, and shook them. I was sure mine was a cricket bat. Virginia expected an easel. On Christmas morning, we rushed downstairs and ripped off the wrapping. Disappointment was tied with a red bow. Two tennis rackets. "Just try it," Mom encouraged. "Maybe you'll like it."

"It's a silly game. I won't play it."

I had no idea that this piece of wood and string would soon become the central icon of my youth, the source of my identity, the one endeavor that gave me any sense of specialness or worth. We made the lawn into a tennis court. Soon we were playing tennis every chance we got. The surface was more like a just-plowed field than a tennis court. The ball could bounce in any direction and usually did, great training in the most fundamental rule of tennis: keep your eye on the ball. Our net was a piece of string. Much of the time, it was impossible to tell if the ball went over or under the string, but that worked well for me, the smallest and weakest player in the family. Our court had no fence around it, but a huge hedge that constantly swallowed the balls. We hit a lot of balls over the hedge too. They rolled down the hill. Pokie, our Sealyham terrier, happy in the role of ball girl, dragged the wayward balls through the ditch, before depositing them, sopping wet and grimy, at the service line, ready for play.

Our family was together at last. I was usually partnered with Dad because he was the best player, with a wicked, untouchable spin. I loved thinking of Dad and me as a team. We laughed and hooted and hollered, tossing our rackets in the air and celebrating after our games with tea and cakes.

Brian, our neighbor on the far side of the hedge, was a year older than me. He was my best, my only chum. After school, we dashed to the railroad tracks and down the bank together, through the thistles, under the trestle bridge, where we sat for hours, watching the huge steam engines roar by. We scratched off sightings from our little blue book with the call number of every locomotive in the U.K. "Loco spotting," we called it. We dreamed of seeing *The Flying Scotsman*, the most famous locomotive of the day, streaking from some distant, moated castle to a highland hideaway where a beautiful princess was held captive. We squatted next to the track and put our ears to the rails and listened for the first distant hum of the engine, a high-pitched whine, then the shimmy of the track. As the train came around the bend, we laid our big copper pennies on top of the track. You had to wait until the last minute, when the train was bearing down, about to flatten you beyond all recognition. If you run before the train comes round the bend, Brian told me, your penny won't carry luck. He'd wait there, right on the track, until the train was so close you could see the engineer, his eyes bulging wildly, screaming at us to get back. I was always the first one to retreat. I was sure Brian was going to get smashed flatter than his penny, but at the last minute, he'd jump out of the way, and then he'd give me a look of such disgust I almost forgot about my penny. We crouched just a couple of feet from the track, still close enough to breathe in the smell of the grease, thrill to the thunder of the wheels, feel the ground shake under us as the cars roared by. Power and manhood and mystery swelled inside us, all together, in one glorious moment.

"I'm going to be an engineer on a train when I grow up," I said to Brian.

The train had passed, and Brian was already back at the track, searching for our pennies, hoping that ours had held tight to the track, so the huge wheels could flatten the coppers thin and wide, shiny and smooth as silk. We picked up flattened pennies—how thin and sleek they'd become!—rubbing our thumbs across our prizes before slipping them into our pockets to feel the heat of the train against our thighs, as if the power of that train was now in our loins.

Then we scrambled back up the bank, slipping and sliding, gripping our pennies, Brian bigger than me, always a few steps in front, and me suddenly screeching, "Aaagh!" My yell stopped Brian as he reached the top. "What is it, Lad? Wha' happened? Don' go tellin' me ya dropped your copper now."

"No, but I got a..."

"Got a what?"

"A pricker."

"Well, toss it."

Brian didn't understand. "I can't. It's stuck in me skivvies."

Brian laughed.

"It's not funny. It hurts."

"Well, shake the bloody thing off, or ya too daft, are ya?"

"I told you I can't. It's all tight in there."

Brian peered down at me from above.

"I can't get it out. I can't."

"Why can't ya? Where is it?"

I was too embarrassed to speak any more of it. I didn't know what the Brits called it and I wasn't about to ask him, but it stung like crazy and I was scared. I was holding it in tight, and dancing about, because I didn't want to cry, but it hurt something awful. When Brian saw where I was holding my hands, he finally understood. "Ah, lad, not just in ya skivvies. You're telling me you got a pricker in your pecker, that's so, isn't it?"

"Yeah, my pecker." I tried to sound cool, as if I knew the word all along.

"Well, then," he said, "They'll have to cut your pecker off."

"No!"

"Or maybe you're needin' your mum to shake your pecker for you."

He didn't sound worried, but I was. When we got to the top of the bank, he asked me an odd question. "D'ya know what a pecker's for?"

I was squeezing my pecker tight as I could, hoping the pricker would drop. "Of course, I do."

"What's it then?" he asked.

Didn't he realize I was dying? "To pee with, of course."

"Ach, no. Lassies pee too, you know, but they have no peckers."

It was true. What he said was true.

"It's so you can poke her." Brian held his finger out,

jerking it in a kind of poking motion. "You poke the lass with your pecker and that makes the baby come out."

"Poke her?" I didn't see how the pecker could poke the baby out, but Brian was older than me, and he knew a lot. "What do you mean? Where?"

"In the bed. They do it in the bed. I heard all about it."

"No, I mean, where? Where do you poke her? In the tummy? That's where they keep babies, you know." In the excitement of this new topic, I forgot briefly about the pricker in my pecker.

"In the ear, lad, don't ya know it?" Brian scoffed. "You poke your pecker in her ear and the baby comes out."

"Where does it come out?"

"Out the mouth." He sounded very certain.

We were quiet as we headed home. My pecker was stinging again, and my mind swirled with questions. I tried to imagine poking a lass in the ear with my pecker, but I couldn't see it. Once home, I rushed upstairs to the bathroom and drank four glasses of water, then I peed until, swoosh, out came the pricker. Huge relief. But I was haunted by what Brian had told me. Is that really what a pecker was for? How could you poke your pecker in a lass's ear? Mine wouldn't fit. There had to be more to this baby making.

The question rattled around until bath time. Mom always ran the water, then let me play around a bit, before she came in to do the scrubbing. I waited until the bath was almost over before I asked. "Is it true that a man pokes a lass in the ear with his pecker to make a baby come out? Does it matter which ear you poke it in?"

Mom froze. Her face reddened. She dropped the soap. "Where did you hear that?"

"Brian says."

She looked around the bathroom, like Brian might be sitting there. "I don't want you playing with Brian any more. I've a good mind to wash your mouth out. Here, dry yourself off." She tossed the towel at me, then turned away. The bathroom door slammed and she was gone. That was the last bath she ever gave me. And the last time I ever talked about sex with either of my parents. Along the line I learned that Brian had a few of the details mixed up.

Not in the ear, Brian. But I'm sure he's figured it out by now.

Chapter 16

It's a month before Christmas. Jennifer and I get over the little incident with Susan in the tent and settle into a routine, together most weekends though we don't live together. I'm hired as executive director of a neighborhood community center in San Francisco's fabled North Beach district, a dream job for me. How I got such a plum job that I am totally unqualified for is a wonder. I worry about how to keep it secret that they hired a hopelessly unqualified guy. On the first day, a soft-voiced midtwenties guy with rich chestnut-colored skin, one of the most handsome men on the planet, knocks on my door. "Just wanted to say hi. My name's Jamal. I work with the kids."

Jamal lives in the Projects, bleak, cinderblock construction public housing. When I meet him, he is lugging two five-foot stuffed bears.

"So what are those for?"

"Presents." Jamal is a man of few words.

"Anyone special?"

"Pookie and Na'thansha."

"Children? Sisters?" I inquire.

"Jus' kids. But they don't get many Christmas presents."

A year has passed since Ashland and the Carl Rogers

workshop. The doubt demons still haunt me, but I've made some progress. I'm living alone in a walk-up apartment, near Lombard Street, San Francisco's famous "crookedest street in the world." The neighborhood center has a mystique about it. It's been around for seventy-five years, teetering on the brink of greatness, something uniquely San Francisco and special, but it's suffered from mismanagement and can't quite break through. I am their new hope. Ha!

When I walk through the door, I stand in the hub of the universe, a building where all the minority and interest groups in San Francisco come together. Come together, but separately. The center is as segregated as a 1950s Mississippi lunch counter. We host a program for seniors (mostly Italian) and a program for youth (African American). We have a medical clinic (all Asian) and two nursery schools (one mostly Asian, the other white), and so on. Every program belongs to a particular ethnic group. I dream of molding it into the melting pot I learned about in eighth-grade US history, seniors finding purpose by helping little children; youth escorting the ill to and from the clinic; festivities where we all swirl in a stew pot of love together, but we are more like a TV dinner served on a compartmentalized plate, little walls to separate the different dishes.

I work hard to keep my doubts at bay, but a year in, I sense my dream fizzling. I bring my doubts with me to work in the morning and take them home at night. I doubt my relationships. I doubt my leadership. I doubt my vision for the center. I dread going to work.

One Friday night, two of our boys, fifteen years old, argue over a record album. I didn't witness the incident, but it's all we talk about. One boy pulled a knife. Three minutes later, the other is dead. Murder on the doorstep gets my attention. I'm not just incompetent—now I have blood on my hands. "What should we do?" I ask Jamal. "I know there's going to be a church service. Should we have a service at the center too?"

Jamal circles around the stillness. "Hmm."

I'd hoped for more than that. "Good idea? Not a good idea? What do you think?"

Jamal stares at his boots. "You the man."

I'm in the center kitchen cooking turkeys with Toni, the fortyish matriarch of the project community. She's wearing a loose-fitting striped top with a scowling cougar's face on the front. The cougar looks like he wants to eat me. When the turkey's ready for tasting, Toni asks me, "What you prefer, light meat or dark?"

Is this a test?

"No prejudice, now."

"How about a slice of each." Ever the diplomat, I am. Toni and I work well together until we don't. I don't know why it falls apart. Maybe because she left her sack-like purse wide open on the counter and she saw that I saw what was inside: a pharmacy, at least thirty vials of pills. Or maybe that has nothing to do with it. Toni is a member of the board. When she's present, she is the center of every storm. She disappears for months, then she resurfaces, followed by her army, "the community," as she calls them. The community expects to be seated at the board table. I take the position that board meetings are for board members. We're tight on space, but Toni and her army are joined at the hip. "The community expects this center to be open longer hours" is Toni's opening gambit at the board meeting.

"Right on, Toni." Mrs. Gatlin, Toni's first lieutenant, glowers.

I shuffle my papers, trying to look like I know what I'm doing. "We're reviewing the medical clinic caseload right now, Toni. Can we talk about the center hours under new business?"

"These kids need a place to go seven days a week. Don't nobody here give a damn about our kids?" No doubt about who this "nobody" is who don't give a damn. Toni looks at the ceiling when she talks, as if she either has, or is expecting, the Lord's blessing on her words.

"Right on, Toni." Mrs. Gatlin glowers.

I wave my arms and squirm in my chair. "We care a lot about these kids, and we want to hear what you have to say, but right now we're—"

"Don't you be pretending you doin' us no favors here." Toni switches to her preacher's voice, a sure sign of trouble. "Our kids needs jobs. Y'all got yo' fancy jobs and homes to go to. These kids ain't got nothin'." Toni stirs all my doubts and my white guilt. She aims for my balls. She waits for the tiny beads of sweat to form around the tip of my nose. It's true, I don't know how to deal with the kids. Or the adults. Or her. I grew up in a family where we were more afraid of personal conflict than polio and the atom bomb combined.

"Right on, Toni." Mrs. Gatlin glowers.

"And typing skills. The girls need learning to type."

I try to smile and cross my legs.

"You supposed to be helpin' them kids. Helpin' them get trained up so they get jobs."

"Right on, Toni." Mrs. Gatlin glowers.

"We tired." Toni opens up her purse and scoops out a

vial of pills as she reloads. "We tired of yo' bull stuff day and night, know what I mean?" Sounds like a question, but it's not. "You better know what I mean." That's what she's saying.

I know. I nod.

Mrs. Gatlin glowers again. "Right on, Toni."

Toni is on a roll. "What you do here all day, anyway, up in yo' big office?" My office is a former broom closet and it's downstairs, but I don't mention this. Toni's been sharpening her mau-mauing tactics, and I'm the designated flak catcher. Truth is, I have no idea how to deal with her. I need an ally.

After the meeting, I find Jamal. "Jamal, I don't know how to deal with Toni. Can you help me?"

Jamal's face goes white. He's caught in the crossfire. He doesn't want to deal with me dealing with Toni. Who can blame him?

"I visited her in her home the other day. She offered me tea, like I was her best friend, but then at the board meetings, she aims for my balls. How can I work with her? I need some advice. What do I say?"

Jamal stares right through his boots. "You the man."

Call me naive, but it's the first time in my privileged white life that I grasped the depth of the racial divide. I thought I was asking for advice, but I had asked Jamal to do the impossible, to cross over to my side. I wanted to grab my high school history books and circle every place where they talked about the melting pot. "It's not the stew inside," I'd tell them. "It's the pot."

I walked the hallways of the center and heard only the echo of my own doubting voice inside my hollow brain. *You are the fraud man, the fraud man, the fraud man.*

But instead of admitting my fears to myself and trying to find help, I try to cover it up with activity. I forget all about my dream of the melting pot. My new goal is to survive.

Over time, I see less and less of Toni. Rumor spreads that she has cancer. She disappears from the scene, and then so do I. But now, thirty years later, Toni still haunts me. I'm writing about her, thinking about her. Why was I ultimately such a flop with the African American community, like we were on competing juries at the O. J. trial? "He's innocent," Toni would have told me. "You can't stand thinking about that black man bein' with that white woman. That's what's messin' with yo' mind."

"I don't like to see anyone, black or white, get away with murder," I would have told her. Or maybe I would have nodded and walked away.

"Right on, Toni." I still hear Mrs. Gatlin glowering in the background.

*

Once a week, I ride the cable car to the end of the line, Powell and Market, a territory in downtown San Francisco owned by drunks, addicts, pimps, and prostitutes. I climb over a body or two and up the dark stairwell to a small second-floor theater, where I join free spirits from across the city gathered to train in a death-defying ritual called improvisational theater. I enjoy the intensity of the stage. I forget about whether they like me or approve of me and throw myself into the moment. If only I could do the same off stage, in life.

"Two guys meet in a bar and discover they have a date with the same woman." That's the prompt we're given. I'm on stage with a big redheaded guy, midtwenties, with a mile-wide smile and deep-set blue eyes. Our mutual "date" is a small-framed woman with long, straight blonde hair and an infectious laugh. We have thirty seconds to plan our skit.

We play off each other. It's fast paced, electric, zany, and fun. The crowd's laughter and applause urge us into ever more outrageous territory. None of us knows where our act is going, but the adrenalin flows. Ten minutes after we finish to generous applause, none of us can remember exactly what we said or did, but we brewed some magic that had never existed before and will never be again. It's the kind of here and now life we're after.

I quickly become best friends with Jon and Val, my friends from the bar in the improv skit. Ever since the Carl Rogers workshop in Ashland, I've been on a quest, to push the boundaries of life as far as I can and to feel the fullness of life within. Jon is on a similar quest, but he's light years ahead of me, the perfect partner for my quest. Jennifer and I, along with Jan, a friend of Jennifer's, pool our resources to buy a duplex Victorian on Eighteenth Street in Noe Valley. Jon, Val, and I move in together in the downstairs unit. Jan and her partner, Gore, live upstairs. Jennifer and I are still cobbled together. She is a frequent visitor, but not a resident. Jan is an Amazon, brazen and raucous, six feet tall, with short, straight black hair, a neck like a goose, and breasts like huge rubber balls bobbing at sea. Gore is twenty years her senior, shaped like a pot-bellied stove from an old Western, and a foot shorter than Jan. They walk down the street like a Mac truck and a pug dog out for a stroll. I try to visualize them in bed, but all I can see is Gore's head lost forever in the bobble of bountiful breasts.

The seventies are a wild and confusing time to live in San Francisco. Drugs are everywhere. Jim Jones is preaching his maniacal powers that will lead to Jonestown, the single biggest loss of American civilian life in a deliberate act prior to 9/11. Patty Hearst is kidnapped, then joins forces with her Symbionese Liberation Army abductors. Pre-AIDS, the gay community thrives. Harvey Milk, the first openly gay supervisor, and Mayor George Moscone are assassinated by a disaffected former policeman. Women's Lib makes it okay for women to ask men out on dates.

We live in the Castro District, the heart of gay San Francisco. The duplex that I share with Jon and Val is a microcosm of the spirit of San Francisco. We set no limits and see no need for any. No mistake is too big to try. I am a caterpillar ready to be a butterfly, but I don't know how to fly. Marshall Tucker's "Fire on the Mountain" is our theme song, playing night and day.

I've experimented with marijuana, and had some far-out experiences with cookies in Greece, but I'm no drug expert and a bit timid. Jon suggests we take a trip together. "Where do you want to go?" I ask.

"Wherever the spirit takes us." Jon's smile takes in the whole world.

"Yes, but…I mean, north, east, south?" West is pretty much out.

"How about straight up?" He pulls out a small, green tab of paper with a purple dot in the middle.

I'm clueless. "What's that?"

"That's your ticket," he says.

"What's our destination?" I ask.

"Wherever you want to go, my friend."

After LSD and I have been formally introduced, I ask the obvious questions. "Where?"

"Here."

"When?"

"Now," Jon says. "It's the only time there is."

"How about tomorrow?"

"Tomorrow," Jon puts his arm around my shoulder, "may never happen."

Soon after we move in together, Jon, Val, and I host a Halloween party. Without a costume at party time, I spot a roll of raffle tickets in the bedroom. I strip naked, wind the tickets around me, head to the party, and fit right in. I approach Joyce, an attractive girl with the most amazing, perfectly shaped breasts. She joins Jon and me on the couch. "That's a wonderful costume," she says. "Can I get a raffle ticket?" I peel off a ticket and hand it to her. She gives it a kiss. A moment later, she's stroking my ticket. Then I notice that Jon has his hand up her dress. Joyce sits impassive through it all, like she's watching Saturday morning cartoons on TV. Jon signals with a tiny eye movement. Nothing is said, but the three of us are soon in bed together. Those breasts! But when I reach for them, they're like rock, solid silicone, I guess it's like making love to a hunk of granite.

*

Joe, an urbane IBMer and new president of the center board, invites us for Thanksgiving dinner. Jon, Val, and I, in Levis and clean underwear, arrive at dusk at Joe and Rebecca's Russian Hill penthouse apartment. Rebecca welcomes us at the door. "So pleased to meet you. Joe told me all about you. I hope you like roast duck with apricot-Szechuan-peppercorn sauce."

We're in time to marvel at their 360-degree view of the city lights bursting to life. Rebecca is dressed in a low-cut formal black velvet dress, with diamond necklace and matching diamond-studded border around the bodice. "De la Renta," she says, her tiny crimson mouth gathered around each word, as if it's being recorded for posterity.

"What did she say?" Jon whispers.

"Something about the rent."

"What do you think a place like this costs?"

That's when I notice the dining room. Crimson table napkins match the stacks of crimson plates and bowls, each place setting like a many-level pagoda. The crimson pagodas match the six tapered crimson candles that rise like Greek columns from silver candlesticks. In the center of the table is a huge tureen with red roses. Crystal glasses—four at each place—finger bowls, and five enormous serving dishes complete the table decor. There's not a square inch of empty space anywhere. A crimson tablecloth matches the fabric in the chairs, which matches Rebecca's crimson lips. I hear Toni's echo in my ear, "Y'all got yo' fancy jobs and homes to go to. These kids ain't got nothin'." She had a point.

Joe's "come here" finger motion summons us to a ten-foot bay window. Six old-style clear milk bottles are lined up outside the window. "My grandmother's eggnog," Joe says with a conspiratorial grin. "Wicked. Rebecca won't touch it. Want to try some?"

Joe grabs a bottle. I grab one of the glasses from the

table, but Rebecca snatches it back before Joe can pour the eggnog. Rebecca polishes the glass with a crimson napkin she has in her pocket for just such a boorish emergency, returns it to the table, then circles the table, adjusting each setting, an inch here or there, before stepping back to admire her work. Joe disappears into the kitchen and returns with other glasses. "Best not to mess with the table," he says.

He's right about the eggnog. The table starts to spin. "Want some more?" Joe asks. Jon and I accept, as Joe disappears to welcome new arrivals.

Jon returns from the bay window with another bottle of eggnog, which Jon and I pass back and forth, foregoing the unnecessary step of pouring it into our glasses. By the time Joe returns, the bottle has but drops left in it.

Other guests arrive, ten or twenty, I've had too much eggnog to count. "Dinner will be ready in half an hour," Rebecca announces. "While we're waiting, let's each tell a story about our most memorable Thanksgiving." Sounds to me like a question out of Miss Manners's Guide to Stress-free Thanksgiving Entertaining, but the round robin starts. I drink more eggnog.

When it's my turn, I'm inspired to talk about the Thanksgiving I spent in Greece with Sally. "So we had invited some Greek friends over to celebrate our American holiday." I pause, trying to remember what happened next. I gaze around Joe and Rebecca's living room, guests poised like China dolls, each with an hors d'oeuvre on a doily on a tiny, crimson plate. The crimson candles on the table start to undulate, like they want to dance, which leads me to Rebecca's hot crimson lips which…oh never mind, I was telling a story about...what was I telling a story about?...Greece. Yes, Greece, and what about Greece?

"So, this was during the stuffed colonels regime. Stuffed colonels, that's what they were, too. This guy, Georgi Papadopolous, his greasy face was everywhere."

"Get on with the story," Joe interrupts. "What happened?"

"The story, okay, that's what I'm doing. See, during the Papadopolous years, dancing on the tables and throwing glasses—Greek traditions that go back to the time of the gods—was illegal. People who did things like that disappeared and weren't heard from for years. Table dancing was risky even in a private house. But at our Greek Thanksgiving party, we closed all the blinds, turned on Nikis Theodrakis—his music was also banned—and then got up on the tables."

"Did you actually dance on the table?" someone asks.

"Of course! It's the Greek way." Suddenly I'm up and starting to dance. I spin once around the crimson table, then stop to offer my other hand to Rebecca's crimson lips. If looks could kill, I'd be staring up at tree roots. Rejected by Rebecca, I invite other guests to join. They decline, but Jon jumps up.

Someone says, "Lucky we're not in Greece. You'd be up on the table now."

It's brilliant. We're so far gone, it's all we need. In seconds, Jon and I are up on the table, stomping our feet and clapping. A couple of Rebecca's crimson pagodas smash to the floor; the flower arrangement topples; when a candle topples over, we deal with the potential hazard efficiently, dousing the flame with champagne. Joe, who's had almost as much eggnog as we have, is laughing and slapping his thighs. "This is the best Thanksgiving in years!"

Rebecca smears her crimson lipstick into a red bandanna across her face.

Soon after Thanksgiving, Joe and Rebecca divorce. They split the crimson candles. Each gets three.

After Joe and Rebecca split up and after three years at the neighborhood center, I reflect on my early dreams of creating the quintessential American melting pot, and realize that I am alone in the pot. Perhaps I've done all the harm I can do; time to move on. As I'm leaving, I approach Jamal, still looking for answers. "What could I have done differently? I ask Jamal.

"You the man," he says.

Chapter 17

I was ten, crouched behind the kitchen door of our house in England, ear pressed against the door, straining to overhear Mom's whispered words: "If we're going to live in England, he needs to do what the English boys do. That means boarding school."

"Some of the blokes at the factory are recommending a new school up in Norwich," Dad said.

Boarding school?! I stumbled around the house, peed, wandered into the bedroom. By the time I got back to the kitchen, Dad had left. Mom was washing dishes.

I tugged at the blue poppies on her pink apron. "I don't want to go to boarding school."

"What makes you think...?" She examined the plate she was scrubbing, turned it over, made a face, put it back in the sink. "It's for your own good, you know."

I was a spindly kid who might be blown away by the wind, my face like a big question mark, an expression I'd picked up from Mom, a bit overwhelmed by life—we both were. A month later, they bought me a tuck box, some new shirts and shorts, and loaded me into the car and off we went, to Ketteringham Hall, a sprawling estate that was once the domain of wealthy gentry, but had been recently converted into a boys' school. "For your own good," Mom said again. So why were there tears in her eyes? In front of the huge doors to the school, she clicked the car door shut, so quiet I could barely hear it, but the sound sliced through me. I watched the taillights disappear through the wrought iron gate.

The entry to Ketteringham Hall was a dark marble cavern. Two suits of black armor, one with a ball and chain, the other with broadsword ready, awesome in their centuries-long silence, guarded entry and exit. So many questions I wanted to ask these armored guards. "How long have you been here? What do I do to fit in? Will they like me?" My voice, a hollow, empty sound, bounced off the marble walls. The suits of armor chose not to share their secrets.

I was ushered upstairs and assigned a bed in a large, narrow room with nine other boys, five metal beds along each side, slippers tucked neatly at the foot of each bed, hospital corners on all the sheets, pillows that looked like they'd never been slept on. In the bed next to me was a tall boy named Harvey, with sandy colored hair and a face that looked like it was ironed flat at birth. Every morning, Nurse Drummond-Towers gave him an injection. His penis was wrapped in rubber tubing. I tried not to stare.

I was soon lugging around textbooks for Latin, Chemistry, French, Geometry, and Algebra, a far cry from what I remembered from school in the U.S., where recess, music and woodworking had dominated my day. Mrs. Giles, wife of the headmaster, whom I quickly dubbed "Wicked Witch of the West," was my French teacher. When I told her I hadn't studied any of these subjects yet in my third-grade class in America, she nodded knowingly, "Here you'll get properly educated."

Childhood was over. I took my books to bed with me at night, disappearing under the covers to memorize lists of French vocab and geometry theorems. I memorized words and symbols, but none of it made any sense to me. I guessed that's what getting properly educated meant. On Friday evenings, all the boys sat together to write letters home.

Dear Mom and Dad,
    I don't like the kipper fish they serve for breakfast here and wish I could have the french toast you made for me. I miss playing tennis with you. How is Pokie?
    Your son,
    Peter

The Wicked Witch of the West frowned at my draft, crumpled it up, and tossed it in the wastebasket. "Such a sneaky little boy, you are. Tell them what you're learning in French. Tell them about this magnificent building. You'll sit here until you get it right." Her puffy fingers lay a fresh sheet of white paper on my desk, then she moved on, down the row.

Mr. Giles, the headmaster, was a bull of a man, with a beet-red face. His head grew directly out of his shoulders. No neck. Rumor was that before starting a school, he'd been a professional boxer. My first conversation with him, two days after I had arrived at school, was devoted to the science of delivering effective whippings. It seemed that Mr. Giles was looking for bottoms to practice on. I decided not to volunteer. Mr. Giles's current weapon of choice was a riding crop that he kept, always handy, on display, hanging eagerly on the wall in his study. "I'm not sure the riding crop stings sufficiently," he confided to me in a moment of tender intimacy. "I'm looking into a cane they call 'The Little Benjamin.' They say it does a jolly good job."

We started each school morning with an assembly. When Mr. Giles entered, we all rose from our seats. "Good morning, Mr. Giles," we sang in unison. He nodded acceptance of our greeting, signaled us to sit, then read the names of the boys who were to report to his study. I glanced around, exhaling in relief when my name was not called. After the assembly, sitting in our classrooms, we heard and counted the swish-whap of the whip. We squeezed our sphincter muscles in solidarity with the exposed bottom that was, at that very moment, advancing Mr. Giles's research on the science of whipping.

One particular assembly the name of every boy in my class was called. "For gross negligence and spelling failure," Mr. Giles proclaimed. Ten minutes later, as we lined up along the wall of his study, I learned that we had all failed the prior day's spelling test. Mr. Giles lectured us on what hopeless students we were, then one by one he brought us forward, instructing us to pull down our pants, bend over and hold the arms of the black wicker chair. I tensed my toes, tried to stop my legs from shaking, but it was no use. I gritted my teeth and waited for the grunt before the blow, whap, and the sting, one, whap, that's two. Whap again and whap. The sting shot down my legs and up into my chest. *I will not cry. I will not.* It was over, but my hands were unable to let go the chair. "Pull up your pants," Mr. Giles ordered. "Next boy." We were dismissed to shuffle down the hallway, back to class, where we stood along the back wall, until we were able to sit.

That night we gathered in the communal shower and compared the bright red welts that snaked across our butts. "Mine's bigger than yours."

"'Tis not. Hey, Simon. Give a look to say whose is bigger."

"Terry's is bigger, but yours is darker red."

"Red's what counts." The welt was my red badge of courage. Some boys had cried. I was proud that I hadn't. For days, I watched the welts change from red to brown, then begin to fade. I twisted in front of the mirror, trying to see the full spread of the welts. I missed them when they were gone. Shame and honor. Fear and pride. Don't ask me to explain.

A month after the spelling-test whipping, we were called out of class for a special assembly. This was something new. The hallways smelled of tension and rumor. Terry had a knowing look on his face: "Someone's going to get it this time."

"Once he was so mad," Terry explained, "he did it in the assembly room, had the boy face his naked bum to the whole school. Ten lashes in front of the whole school. You don't forget that."

But something was different this time. We sensed it the moment we walked in. The curtains were drawn. No music. Mr. Giles was seated already on stage, his head bowed. He waited until everyone was in place, then he walked slowly forward, none of the usual swagger. "I have sad news." He pulled a handkerchief from his pocket and wiped his nose, sniffed before continuing. We searched for clues. Silence hovered. Mr. Giles cleared his throat. "The king is dead."

All around the room, sobs broke out, some wild and uncontrolled, some muffled, wails that looped around us, then hung, suspended in the air above the doors and windows. One boy collapsed on the floor. I buried my head in my hands, feigning sorrow, hoping to blend in. The king meant nothing to me.

We filed back to class, all the boys in somber silence. Except me. I whistled. It was something I did, no special meaning. A hand gripped my shoulder. "What's this whistling, I hear?"

"Yes, sir, it's a song I like."

"The king is dead. And you're whistling." Mr. Giles gripped me harder, his face reddening.

"I'm American," I explained. "He's not my king."

"You'll jolly well learn respect." He took me by the ear and marched me to his study. The swish of the cane again. "And one more for the king," he said. "May he rest in peace. And another. Some respect, you cheeky little boy."

I slinked back to class. *I'm a cheeky little boy. I didn't respect the king. I wouldn't mind having a king, so I could wail like the rest of them. It's different to be an American. Why don't we have a king? We have a president. Is the president our king? Are you supposed to cry when the president dies?*

I was confused and embarrassed at the king's assembly, but shamed by what showed up around Rupert. Rupert was the class clown, not a bad kid, but mischievous. Mr. Giles regularly smacked Rupert's butt with his trusty riding crop, but to no avail, so he developed a new strategy. Mr.

Giles showed us the big, olive green "Rupert book" that he stored in the closet next to the cane. When we observed Rupert breaking a rule, we were to write the date and time of the sighting in the Rupert book. Five infractions earned Rupert "three of the best." Rupert couldn't win. We quickly become obsessed with tracking his sins. One rule, for example, was that no one was to walk within six inches of any wall. The intent was to keep boys' filthy hands away from the lovely clean walls, but in fact, the rule was impossible to obey, some of the halls being so narrow that you couldn't walk down them without being too close to one wall or the other. We weren't bothered by such details. We followed behind Rupert with a ruler in hand so as not to miss any infraction. I am ashamed to say that I cooperated in this ridiculous persecution, even though I knew full well what a cruel hoax the whole thing was. Why did I do this? Why do people collaborate with evil? I got some immediate feeling of power, I guess. There was someone I could look down on. Rupert was—unbelievably—lower on the ladder of acceptance than me.

Rupert, I hope, moved on, but years later, part of me was still stuck, back there with Rupert. Being unable to forgive myself was a more painful, more enduring punishment than the beatings.

*

One Saturday in spring, the sun shone with self-righteous intent. The sun rarely shone in spring in England. To celebrate the occasion, the Wicked Witch of the West marched a half-dozen of us boys to the outdoor shower, which was hidden from view by a high wall on two sides.

"Now, boys, it's time for some fun in the sun. Take off your clothes, everyone."

We glanced about. *Take off our clothes. What does she mean?*

Nurse Drummond-Towers, her nose oily and glistening in the sun, stood behind the witch. She held a small black box. Witch whispered something in Nurse's ear.

"Chop chop." Witch Giles clapped her hands, and Nurse Drummond-Towers squatted down low with her box.

Uncertain but trained to obey, we unbuttoned our shirts, then stood in doubt; what next? We were stripped to the waist, our modesty shielded only by our knee-length shorts and long gray socks.

"Jolly good, now the rest of it. Chop chop. Feel that sun all over. We want to tan evenly, don't we?"

I slipped off my shorts and socks. Nurse Drummond-Towers snooped around us, like a child searching for candy. "Off with the undies now. Everyone. Extra pudding tonight for all those who let the sun tan every inch of your little bodies."

Who would go first? We tugged awkwardly at our underwear, bent slightly, lifted one leg, then the other, bunched up our undergarments to cover our privates, and turned away. "Don't be bashful," Witch Giles exhorted us. "Toss the undies over here." She pointed. "The sun is over this way. Let's give those little peckers a chance to shine, shall we."

Nurse lowered the black box. A few clicks. She crouched low for a better angle. Nurse and the witch stood next to each other, giggled and pointed. "Look at Ian's, will you? Magnificent. And poor Robert's, so tiny you can barely see it. How will he ever—"

Instinct turned me away from the camera. The witch was on me in a second. "Now, Gibb, let's have a nice big American smile, and show us that big American pecker of yours, come on now, this is no time to be bashful."

Nurse clicked a few last shots for posterity. "Our time in the sun is over for today. Put your skivvies back on. No talking until you're back inside," Mrs. Giles commanded.

The sun disappeared behind a cloud as we stood in line to head back to the dormitory. The photo shoot was finished. I buried the memory deep inside, deep in the rubble, where it rested untouched for decades.

*

One dark and cold night after dinner, I had endured all I could take of Ketteringham Hall, so I snuck out the back door of the school and headed for town. I had no idea how to get to town, or what I would do when I got there. A headlight swung by. A dog barked. My heart thumped. I had no money and no plan, but I was running away. I wanted to go home. About fifteen minutes beyond the gate, I heard a car slowing down behind me. No time, no place to hide. I froze. The car stopped. I recognized Mr. Giles voice.

"Get in the car." He opened the door for me. How did he know? I got in. Not another word was exchanged between us, but I could feel the beating already. Would it be in front of the whole school? Would I be the one they talked about next? How my butt had so many welts it looked like a fire engine. Ten lashes? Fifteen? Would I be able to take it, or would I collapse on the floor? Would it be tomorrow at the assembly? Or maybe even tonight?

We returned to school and entered through the big

marble hallway, between the two suits of armor. Mr. Giles stopped. He looked down the hallway, in the direction of his study.

"Don't ever do that again," he said. "Now go to bed."

By the end of the year at Ketteringham Hall, Mom and Dad had decided to move back to the United States. As the senior class in the school, my classmates were all moving on to the next level. The Wicked Witch of the West sat at the teacher's desk, her hair pulled back in a tight bun held by a dark brown ribbon. She eyed us one by one, like we were pastries on a shelf, discussing where each boy was headed. When she came to me, she stopped, perhaps unsure what to say, but after a moment's thought, she recovered. "So, Gibb. You're returning to the United States. That's the end of you."

Chapter 18

1977. I've been living in the San Francisco Bay Area for two jobs, three years, and four girlfriends. I endure Gestalt groups, have my aura fluffed and my body Rolfed. I regress back to my past life as a slave buried alive in the second century BC; "That's why you are still searching for god in this life," my past-life reader tells me. "With a series of five readings, I can free you from the past and release you into the bliss you were meant to inhabit in this life."

"Not now, thanks." My Leo, so I'm told, is aligned with lucky Jupiter and thrilling Uranus. All this is fine, but my doubts are growing. I'm no closer to knowing who I am, or where I'm going, or who I'm going with.

I move into a communal home, seven of us in a bucolic, rambling estate with a wraparound porch that reminds me of Mayma and Grandpa's summer home. But that's where the resemblance ends. My new home is as far from my conservative roots as is possible. Clothes are optional. Dope is plentiful. We celebrate that no one in the house works a straight job. I merge into the miasma. I've left the Community Center job. Daniel and I set up a small home remodeling business that we call Hillside Builders, so named because we live on Hillside Avenue. A lady phones one day to ask if we build on hillsides. "Hillsides? Of course!" Thus is born a niche market that feeds and clothes me for a while. But I feel like a pinball, ricocheting off bumpers. I drop into a hole for three hundred points. Bells ring; lights flash. It has its moments, but deep down I feel superficial.

I smoke a fat joint and sink into the bathtub, the water as hot as I can run it. If I last to the count of ten, then...then what? Four. Five. I hold out to six, grab the tub and push myself up, lifting my feet onto the sides of the tub, my body suspended above the cauldron. How hot can I tolerate? When will I have sufficiently purified myself? Not yet? Okay, I drop back in again. Such pleasure in pain. This time I last to eight. I am red meat.

I slide in and out as the water cools. I bake for an hour, watching my knees float, following a crack in the wall, letting images and a mood roll over me. The mood is ugly.

I am thirty-five years old, no longer a kid, still trying to answer youthful questions: What do I believe? What do I want to do with my life? Mom told me I could do anything I wanted to, but what do you do if you don't know what you want to do, and I don't? In third grade I was certain I wanted to be a baseball player. Baseball player morphed into tennis player. Once I realized the limitations of my athletic ability, I moved on. I fantasized about becoming a priest, a psychiatrist, a diplomat, a writer, a professor, but I never troubled myself to learn the first thing about preaching, counseling, diplomacy, writing, or professing. Now I define myself as a wanderer, an explorer of the spirit. It sounds good. Until you scratch beneath the surface. I am more like a middle-aged adolescent, in no hurry to grow up, wasting away under a cloud of marijuana and new-age platitudes.

I climb out of the tub, check my naked body in the mirror. Red, shriveled skin, misty eyes, right shoulder and back aching from old tennis injuries. A wild head of curly dark hair. Who is this man who retreats to the bathroom night after night, smokes a joint, and tries to boil away his misery in the tub? I don't have a family. Family, hah, I don't even have a girlfriend. I don't own a home. I have no career. I lost my soul thirty years ago and never found it again.

I'm a hippie, but I'm not even a real hippie. I don't have a beard, I don't wear beads, and I don't own any bell-bottom pants. I don't say, "Far out!" I don't have an old lady, and I don't own a big dog. I tell myself that I'm fighting for my freedom, but who is my jailer? Only one person who prevents me from being free. Everywhere I go, there he is.

I am free to fear. I fear everything: conformity, a wasted life, putting myself in too small a box, missing my destiny. While I search for destiny, life is passing me by. It's true I can make up a reasonable-sounding resume: I graduated from a good college where I was vice president of the student union; I've taught high school and university, had a responsible overseas position with the state department, managed a well-respected nonprofit. I spent four years in the air force, acted in USO theater productions, taught languages in Greece, and travelled around Europe. I'm quite fluent in two foreign languages and can bumble along in another.

"Ooh, wow," people say when I recite my bio. "That's cool. You're so lucky."

I don't feel lucky. I don't feel cool. I'm a misfit, that's

what. My life is a labyrinth of dark, smudgy days and darker, rat-turd nights. I dive deeper into my "former life" as a Roman slave, the life I learned about in my past-life regression. I refine the story, make up details. I was handsome and intelligent, captured in battle, enslaved, brutally treated, then discovered by the empress, who draws me into her bed. I defy the emperor, daring death in the name of passion and freedom. Discovered, mocked, sentenced to death, I show no fear. I will be memorialized in song and story. A hero I am, a noble victim. I delight in the joy of the self-righteous.

Interrupted dreams. Someone is kicking at the bathroom door. "You've been in there for an hour. Get out of the bathroom, man. I need to brush my teeth."

I pull the plug, wrap myself in a towel, and unlock the door. Michael is standing outside in his blue Mickey Mouse skivvies, a joint in his hand. He offers me a toke. I shake my head, brush by without a word, shamble the few feet to my bedroom, close and lock the door, and collapse naked on the bed.

My stash is never far away. I reach for a big fat joint and strike a match. The fog descends. I cover the pain, at least for now. Alone in my room, I get high each night, without having to reckon with anyone. I pull out my sketch journal and a pen. I draw when I'm stoned, wild, free-flowing drawings, a line leads to a shape that leads to an image that leads to a line that suggests a...I stop to wow. I have created a map to unlock the mystery of life.

But when I inspect my drawing in the morning, I see it as a jumble of lines and shapes unlocking nothing but the chaos of my own mind.

I withdraw increasingly from my housemates. I can't wait for dinner to be over. I don't want to be there. I don't want to be anywhere. Night after night, I repeat the bathtub ritual, but no amount of scrubbing will get me clean. I am at the midpoint of my life expectancy. Perhaps the best years are past. Several friends from college are already dead. I drift into fantasy again, this time imagining myself at the Pearly Gates, met by St. Peter clutching the Big Book of Life. "Hmm, not much to show for yourself."

I hang my head in shame. "No."

"Why not?"

"Too many choices. I couldn't settle on anything."

St. Peter smirks. He's seen others from the Club of Doubt, I'm sure.

I've been given more than my share of opportunities. I wasn't abandoned, starved, or abused. I was fed, supported, and educated. Loved, albeit in an oblique way. I have none of the usual excuses. So why am I so filled with doubt? Why so lost?

St. Peter closes the Big Book. "I'll give you one more chance. Make something of your life, or…" He doesn't finish his sentence. He doesn't have to. I was brought up Catholic. I know all about eternal consequences.

I pick up another joint, start to light it, but something stops me. I blow out the match and cast the joint aside, lie still, close my eyes, let my mind drift. I face myself as an old man. I am sixty, seventy, eighty. The age doesn't matter. I am stuffed in an armchair, morning coffee spilled down my shirt, mouth hanging open like a fish after the hook is removed, the smell of urine on my clothes, my eyes glazed and still.

I remember Dad, whom I loved so much in his earlier years, before he gave up and left Mom. Or she left him. I was never sure which. Doesn't matter now. He came back. Or we came back. And we settled into the same life we'd lived before, a life in gray. I thought that was all there was. And now, in what should be the prime of my life, am I reliving my parents' lives? Were their lives as limited as I see them? From outside, their marriage looked fine. No yelling or screaming; no abuse; it was polite; few overt arguments; the normal amount of passive-aggressive bickering. My parents weren't philanderers, drunks, drug addicts, sexual predators, convicted felons, compulsive gamblers, pimps, prostitutes, bipolar narcissists, or any of the other usual culprits. They were kind, decent people who led quiet, law-abiding lives, cared for their children, respected their parents, played golf, watched TV, and paid their taxes. So what's wrong with that?

Nothing. Everything.

My parents met in 1934 thanks to one of those rolls of the dice that come along when you're least expecting it and change everything. Mom was vacationing in Hawaii with her sister Nellie, already the mother of two daughters. The day before they were scheduled to return to the mainland, one of the nieces came down with chicken pox. Travel plans were scuttled. The next day, the British fleet sailed into port. There was a dance, and the rest, as they say, is history. Except it almost wasn't. Mom was a proper lady, accustomed to the rules of Washington society. She couldn't go to a dance unescorted.

Mom's sister Nellie applied gentle pressure. "You're thirty-two. It's time, you know." So she went to the dance.

They met. They talked. They danced. He was dashing and romantic in his dress-white uniform. He explained how he was now a lieutenant who had entered the Royal Navy at thirteen, finished school at Osborne Naval School on the Isle of Wight, off the south coast of England, then joined the second class of pilots ever trained by the British navy. He loved flight school, despite its grisly record. He was one of the first pilots to fly open cockpit biplanes off aircraft carriers. Dangerous business back in those days—50 percent of his class died in training-related accidents before graduation. He talked about the thrill of flying with the wind in your hair, flying into the wild blue yonder, with "visibility unlimited." At sixteen, he'd witnessed the at-sea surrender of the German Fleet at the end of WWI. He was brave. He was handsome. He was worldly. He'd been everywhere. Her heart opened. She wanted to kiss him, but she never let on.

They exchanged addresses. Two days later, she waved good-bye to her pilot as the British fleet weighed anchor. All those handsome young sailors on deck waving, she couldn't even tell exactly which one was her sailor, but her eyes teared up. She tried to imagine what it might be like to marry a foreigner, a navy man, a man who risked his life every day in a small, open cockpit. This was long before Snoopy. Back at the hotel, she took out a piece of stationery. In dark blue—navy blue—ink, she wrote "Mrs. Charles Gibb" over and over. At first it felt awkward, but practice made it natural. Then she tore the paper into small pieces and hid them at the bottom of the wastepaper basket where her sister Nellie would never find them.

Back in Washington, over a five-year span, chatty but

infrequent letters and postcards arrived from Ceylon, Barbados, Singapore, China, Canada, Trinidad. She hung a world map in her room and ran her finger across the map, searching for his location. She stuck a pin when she'd located him, knowing that he'd probably already moved on to some other exotic place. By now most of her girlfriends were married. She was not lacking for beaus (as she called them), but late at night, she often reached under the bed for the shoebox of letters and cards from the dashing young British lieutenant, from wherever in the world, from a ship, from a place, from a man she barely knew but was irresistibly drawn toward. She was always first to check the mail. Once or twice he enclosed a pen-and-ink drawing he'd done of his ship or his airplane. He drew so well. He was so talented, but his letters were mostly postcards, open for all the world to read. They were all signed, "Yours, Otie." Then one day in February 1938, a rap on the front door, a boy from Western Union: "Telegram for Mary Louise Johnson."

Fear tore through her. The worst news always comes by telegram. She held the telegram in her shaking hand, went into the sitting room, and shut the door. She closed her eyes and sat in prayer for minutes before she dared open it. She took the silver letter opener and slowly sliced open the top of the envelope. The message was brief, two lines. "Home on leave in England for two months STOP Will you marry me? STOP Details follow STOP Yours, Otie."

She jumped up, shrieked so loud her parents came running. She waved the telegram at them. "What should I do?"

There were questions. "Where would you live?" "What about his family, are they our kind of people?" "How much will he be gone?" "Would you travel with him?" "What about children?" "Has he agreed to bring them up Catholic?" "What if another war breaks out?" "Can he support you?" "Do you know what a lieutenant earns?"

These were good questions. She had no good answers.

She told her parents most of what she knew about him. Otie was his nickname, derived from "El Otro," Spanish for "the other one." He was the younger brother, born in 1902, in central Mexico, where his British parents were ranching. She didn't tell them that his father had been murdered in Mexico, at the start of the Mexican revolution. Otie had never told her the full story, but he hinted—or she sensed—that it had something to do with some señoritas he shouldn't have been messing with. After his father's death, Otie scampered back to England, where he was raised by his maternal grandmother until he was sent away to navy school at thirteen.

Mayma listened quietly to hours of discussion, then gave her bottom line. "It's your life. You have to do what you think is best."

Grandpa was dubious. "Why did his parents leave England?" "What was the full story behind his father's murder?" "Why hasn't he come to Washington to visit you?"

She barely slept, wrestling the question back and forth for days. She'd always done what her father thought best, but was his opposition now based on legitimate reasoning, or was he reluctant to see his favorite daughter leave Washington to marry a foreigner with an ambiguous past?

"You have to answer the telegram," her mother coaxed. "The poor man is waiting."

As soon as she thought yes, then all the arguments

against it crowded in, but when she thought no, her heart cried out so she could barely breathe. When she thought of him, all she could see was his smile, like a warm fire on a cold winter's night, and her heart yearned to curl up next to him.

When her father took her to the Western Union office, she was still unsure what she would say. The clerk gave her a yellow form to complete, "Print. Exactly as you want the telegram to read," he said. "Plus your name and address and the addressee's name and address." She took the form over to a table and hovered the pen over the form. She looked up at the wall clock, then at her father. She closed her eyes, breathed deeply and wrote.

"I accept."

My mother flew to England with her father for a small wedding in Heacham, Norfolk, in June 1938. They began their married life together but were soon separated when Dad went to sea for months at a time. Mom lived alone in England. In 1940, my sister Virginia was born in England. Two years later, with Mom now back in the United States living with her parents, I arrived. Dad missed both births.

*

Back in my communal home in San Anselmo, California, I lie on the bed and think about how I came into this world, how similar and yet how different my life is from my parents'. I want to grab hold of life and say, "What is the possibility here? What can I make of this?" Not that I follow through, but the thought is there. Dad always seemed so unambitious to me, so quick to accept whatever came his way. But who am I to talk? Mr. Fulfillment, here.

Mr. Happy. Mr. Success. More like the King of Doubt. Still, now thirty-five. I am too hip for the straights and too straight for the hipsters; too old for the future-leaders club, too young for the wise-elder group; too well established for the diaspora, too poor for the gentry of Marin County. Everyone wants a tribe to belong to. My parents had each other. Sort of. I have a history of stuttered relationships, transitory jobs, and quixotic crusades. I am the late bloomer who never bloomed.

I migrate between anhedonia, a kind of passive joylessness, and a more debilitating depression that robs me of ambition, motivation, and any sense of accomplishment or meaning. As I drive down Highway 101, the beautiful San Francisco Bay turns dark and menacing. Sailboats that had once been a symbol of serenity become lost, floundering specks, tossed about on hungry waters. Monsoonlike rains drench the Marin hills, carving gorges, undermining foundations, sending houses—and my delicate psyche—sliding down the hillside. I smoke more and more marijuana, hoping to escape. I too am buried in the mud.

Jennifer, Jan, and I sell the Victorian house we'd owned together and make a tidy profit. Now, three of us from the San Anselmo house pool our resources to buy a few acres of land, about a two-hour drive North of Marin in Sonoma County. The undeveloped land feeds our back-to-the-land fantasy and is a good spot to grow some pot. Every two weeks, we drive up Highway 1, the necklace of highway that runs along the California Coast. Inland are the rolling green hills, cows munching on green grass, and lichen-covered fences. On the coast side, the battle for dominion rages between land and water. Prehistoric boulders rise out of the water like ancient gods. Fields of yellow-orange California poppies broadcast hope everywhere. The biweekly drive awakens both my loneliness and my romantic dreams. Possibility dances before me one minute. The next I slump into the brokenness of my own life.

I watch a red-winged blackbird emerge from the fog, back into it, visible, invisible, swooping across the road, climbing, diving, hiding, as if to awaken me to some deep mystery, or is it just to boast? I follow her brilliant scarlet and yellow epaulet. She commands the stage with a brief dance, soars upward until she is a tiny speck, swoops back down, climbs, dives, leaps, then lingers, delighting herself, delighting me, shunning the sea in favor of the marsh, settling on a fencepost, where she drinks a tiny drop of water that has been waiting there for her. I am jealous of her freedom. She is more like the wisps of cloud than the rocks. She puffs out her colors, fans her tail, and celebrates the moment in song.

I sit up a little straighter, feel a tickle of flame, a breath of hope inside. Life is more than random noise. I am here for a reason. I must find that reason.

My eyes calm. I take a deep breath. I have been fighting for so long to escape my demons. As if I could somehow be free of my own nature. I have tried so hard to please others, I barely know what it means to please myself. This blackbird flies into her song, not from it. Perhaps I shouldn't be running from my fears, but into them.

I look to the sky for the answer. The blackbird swoops overhead. Sing, she says. Sing.

Chapter 19

I was twelve when we left England for the last time and returned to Washington, DC, once again to live with Mayma and Grandpa. Dad was with us this time. He'd given up the idea of living in England. I was happy. He was not.

Mom enrolled me at Georgetown Prep, a Catholic middle and high school run by Jesuits that specialized in preparing Catholic boys to walk and talk like saints-in-training. When I enrolled, being Catholic meant little to me. I had been going to church for years, with no idea of what church was all about. It was something we did on Sunday. I watched Mom kneel and pray, bending low and burying her head in her hands. Her hands shook. Was she visited by the same demons who tormented me?

In my new Catholic school, behind every teacher's desk, from high on every wall, Jesus looked down from the cross.

Mr. McGrath, our wavy-haired seventh-grade teacher was in training to become a Jesuit priest. We called him "Mister." A constant gum chewer, he wore a long black robe, his collar backward. Rosary beads dangled down the front of his robe. At the beginning of the year, I wondered why a man would want to wear a black dress. By the end of the year, I wanted to be a priest. If I were a priest, then I'd know what to say and do too, and my doubts would disappear in fear and trembling.

In English grammar, we studied the parts of a sentence. Example: "Jesus died for our sins." Explanation: "'Jesus' is the subject of the sentence. 'Died' is the verb. 'For our sins' is a prepositional phrase that explains why Jesus had to die." In math, we studied long division. "If God had two hundred eighty-eight angels, and he wanted to divide them equally into sixteen groups, how many angels would be in each group?" In English lit, we read the lives of the saints. My favorite was St. Casimir, whose miraculous powers helped the blind to see, the lame to walk, the sick to heal, and the dead to return to life. I wanted to do such things too.

Mr. McGrath announced it was time for confession. The class paraded to the chapel, a row of stony faces, silent and somber, unlike any group of boys I'd ever seen. I had no idea what confession was, but I wasn't about to admit what a clueless Catholic I was. *Confession must be talking with God about what I'd done wrong.* That's not so hard, I thought. We lined up along the marble wall of the chapel. Classmates disappeared behind the black curtain, where they remained hidden for four or five minutes—chatting with God, I assumed—before they emerged with downcast eyes and serious gait, knelt in a pew, hands folded together in prayer position for about five minutes.

When my turn came, I pushed the curtain aside and found myself in a small, dark cubicle with a kneeling cushion on the floor and a narrow shelf at waist level, for my elbows. I knelt on the cushion, listening to muffled voices from the darkness. I assumed I'd be alone with God. *Does God actually talk out loud?* I heard a louder rustling noise, then the outline of a head emerged from the darkness in front of me. *Is this the Almighty himself?* Before I could run, the head mumbled, "How long has it been since your last confession, my son?"

"God. Is that you?" I asked.

"Just call me Father."

This was not my father. Whoever it was cleared his throat. "Do you have something to say to me? How long since your last confession, my son?"

"Ten minutes?" My voice quaked. "Dad? Is that you?"

"Father. Call me Father, not Dad." Squirming and more throat clearing from the far side of the black cave. "Have you been to confession before, my son?"

I smelled trouble. "Not exactly."

His voice lowered an octave. "What grade are you in?"

"Mr. McGrath's seventh grade, Lord."

"Ask Mr. McGrath to instruct you in how to make a good confession. Say two Hail Marys and two Our Fathers for the forgiveness of sins. Go now."

I slipped out through the curtain, full of shame. I had failed—in front of God and everybody. I headed into a pew and buried my head in my hands. What was that all about? *Had I actually been talking to God? What do I do now? How long should I stay in the pew? Will God tell anyone? Can I keep it a secret? Am I headed for Hell?* I felt a hand on my shoulder. When I opened my eyes, I was staring into the crucifix that hung at Mr. McGrath's side. "Follow me."

Back in the classroom, Mr. McGrath told me to sit. "Father Dougherty was not amused by your performance today."

"Who is Father Dougherty?"

"The priest who heard your...who was in the confessional."

"It wasn't God?"

Mr. McGrath stopped chewing his gum. He narrowed his eyes, rose slowly and walked over to me. "May you burn in Hell if you ever...ever, ever...mock the Lord."

"I'm not mocking—"

We began my instructions for how to make a good confession that afternoon. "God knows everything," Mr. McGrath drilled me over and over. "Even your most private thoughts. Confession is your chance to wipe the slate clean. Do you play Monopoly? Confession is like a 'Get Out of Jail Free' pass, only the jail is Hell. Without the sacrament of confession, you would be doomed to suffer eternity in Hell. Think of it. Forever and ever, no end, eternity amidst the damned, burning in the fires of Hell. You don't want that, do you?"

"No, Mister."

"You must confess everything, even your most private, sinful thoughts and deeds."

"Yes, Mister."

"You cannot hide anything from God, do you understand?"

"No, Mister. I mean, yes, Mister."

After three lessons, I was ready to confess again, but before that happened, life got complicated. I was riding the bus to school in the morning. A blonde girl, about my age, stood on the corner, waiting for her bus, holding a stack of books tight against her tummy, her luscious, budding breasts peeking out over her books, cookies on the shelf, just out of reach. As I watched, she turned away and walked farther back on the sidewalk. I followed her beautiful round bottom and the line of her underpants, how it surged and fell with each step she took. By the time our bus pulled away, I was in love. She bobbed around inside my mind for the rest of the bus trip. Later, when we went to chapel, she was all I could think about. Then, the worst thing possible, a tightening in my pants. I'd had a boner in the bathtub and sometimes I even woke up at night with one, but never in church. I thought of Mr. McGrath's words, "God knows everything. Hell is forever." I lay the missal in my lap to hide the bulge. I prayed that the boner would go away. It grew. I should be thinking about God, but I was thinking about my boner and the girl at the bus stop. I couldn't possibly tell the priest about the boner. Or the girl.

Later that day, Mr. McGrath told me it was time for my first real confession. I almost wet my pants as I knelt behind the black curtain. The priest pulled back the screen. "Bless me Father, for I have sinned." I confessed a couple of minor sins, then fell into silence.

"Is that all, my son?"

I closed my eyes and there she was, her sweet breasts peering over her books. The boner rose to greet her. Was this God's way of torturing me?

"Have you had any impure thoughts, my son?"

"No, Father."

"None?"

He knows. *He wants sins. I'll give him sins.* I made up sins, as many as I could think of. "I stole money from my sister. I got angry at my mother. I kicked the dog. I lied to my father about finishing my homework." *I'm sinning at this very moment, making up lies to satisfy you, to give you something to forgive me for.* "I was mean to my friend," I continued. "I said a bad word. I was daydreaming in Mass. I deliberately broke my mother's favorite glass, and I hid her earring where she wouldn't ever find it, and—"

"Impure thoughts," he interrupted. "Have you had impure thoughts?"

How does he know? I shook my head.

"Well, that's quite enough for one confession," the priest interrupted.

I was out of the confessional before he'd finished his instructions. I knelt in the pew the way I'd watched the others. *Was it five Hail Marys and three Our Fathers or three Hail Marys and five Our Fathers? Oh, shit, I can't remember. Oh, shit, if God knows everything, then he knows I just said "shit." Twice. He knows I lied in confession. Lying in confession, that's surely a mortal sin. If I die now, I'm going to Hell. I have to go back to confession. But I'm going to Hell because I went to confession. And I didn't tell him about the boner. But I couldn't. Oh, shit. There I go again. Every time I think "shit" and think that I said "shit" that's two shits. How many shits before you're sent permanently to Hell?*

When I returned to class, Mr. McGrath asked me if I had completed my confession. "Yes, Mister."

"Did you confess all your sins?"

I thought about all the extras I'd thrown in for good measure. "Oh, yes, Mister."

"Mortal sins and venial sins?"

"Yes, Mister."

"Did the priest absolve you from your sins?

"Yes, Mister."

"And you said your penance?"

"Yes, Mister."

Mr. McGrath smiled. "Then you have completed your first real confession. You are at peace, free from sin. Should you die now, you are prepared for Heaven."

I didn't die and I didn't tell him about my shits. I shuffled back to my desk, prepared for Heaven perhaps, but less at peace than I was before my confession. For now, I didn't question the priest's power to forgive me.

We had an hour of religious instructions every day. In quick succession after my first confession, I was confirmed, then made my first communion. "You're three years late for your first communion," Mr. McGrath told me. I understood. I was bad.

Much of my Catholic instruction consisted of writing out and memorizing pages of Q and A from the little red catechism book. With the help of the catechism, things became clear. Good and Evil lined up on opposite sides of the room. Prayer was the answer to all of life's problems. Whenever we heard a siren outside, we halted whatever we were doing to say a prayer. My right hand scratched at my forehead, then to the stomach, before drawing an imaginary line from left shoulder to right. The sign of the cross—at least twice an hour, but I was swept up in the mystery and the clarity of it all, the comfort of knowing that God was there, and that everything I could ever need to know was in The Book.

Doubt was not part of the catechism. Finally I had answers.

It was football season. Before the game, our team knelt together outside the chapel, praying for God's guidance on the gridiron. God must not be so busy, I thought, if he had time to worry about who won a high-school football game.

We won the game. God had time for football. God watched out for our team.

If the football team could ask God for victory, then I could ask Him for favors too. I was excited about playing football. It seemed that next to being a priest, being a football player was about as close as one could come to being a hero, and I wanted to be a hero. I'd skipped a grade when I began school at Georgetown Prep. I was self-conscious about being one of the smallest in the class, but I felt big when I put on shoulder pads. I prayed to God to make me a really good football player, and I was confident he would. But after two weeks of practice, the buzz was suddenly all about "the cut."

"What is the cut?" I asked.

Teammates glanced disbelievingly at me. Tony, a small boy like me, understood. "It's when you find out you didn't make the team."

"I'll make the team," I said. "God is watching out for me."

Tony shrugged. "If you're no good, you get cut."

After class, we went to the locker room to change for practice. There, tacked to the door, was a list of names. "The following boys will play on the seventh-grade team. To those who didn't make it, thanks for trying out. Come back next year." I read down the list, down to the Gs. Past the Gs. Back up again. My name was not there.

"But, God, you promised." Then it occurred to me that I'd asked, but God hadn't really promised. The whole God relationship became more complicated.

"What do we do now that we're cut?" I asked Tony.

"We watch."

The cut introduced me to a new way of being in the world, what Mom called the star system. If you're a star, you get to play. If not, you don't. I sat on the sidelines that day and tried to make sense of it. If you can't play, how do you get to be good? You get good by practice. But I can't practice because I was cut. Even at age twelve, I recognized that there was something very off about such a system.

In spring, I tried out for tennis. This time I made the team. I was the only seventh grader, the youngest in the school on a varsity team. Being on the tennis team wasn't like being on the football team, but it didn't matter that much to me. I took a play out of the football team's playbook and prayed to God for assistance on the court. "Lord, help me win these next two points and I'll say ten Hail Marys tomorrow instead of the usual five." When we won, I knew it was because God was on our side. Mostly we lost. I never stopped to question why.

I became a Catholic zealot. I thought about God first thing in the morning, and dreamed about God at night. I ate breakfast, lunch, and dinner with God. Mr. McGrath explained how a few exceptionally holy people experienced stigmata, the spontaneous appearance of wounds and blood on their hands and feet on Good Friday, in memory of the crucifixion wounds of Jesus. For days before Good Friday, I prayed that I would have the stigmata. First thing in the morning and last thing at night, I examined my hands for signs of blood. Alas, no blood. I was not holy enough. I redoubled my efforts, wore out the knees on my pants. Still no blood.

Being religious at Georgetown Prep was the way to fit in. After being such an outsider in England, I was ready to shave my head to be accepted. Being Catholic gave me, for the first time in my life, a way to be an insider. We were the one true church. Non-Catholics, Christian and non-Christian, were heretics who would never sit at the right hand of God. We knew the truth. No other religion did. We alone were headed for an eternity of bliss in Heaven with Jesus. I imagined myself at the banquet table. Jesus was there, and so were Mom and Dad and Virginia. The whole thing looked remarkably like the Last Supper. The church gave me a platform of certainty to stand on, stark contrast to my world of doubt. Right and wrong, good and evil needed no further debate.

Of course, there was a price to pay. The priests talked about grace and love, but they quickly moved on to fear and punishment. I was scared to death of spending eternity in Hell. I had nightmares in which I saw myself writhing in the flames. Hell, they said, was hotter than the sweltering heat waves of a Washington summer. Hell was not for a minute or an hour or even a month or a year, but foreverandeverandever. I obsessed over the idea of an eternity in Hell. I prayed diligently and struggled to control my sins. I made progress. A typical confession now took only minutes, but controlling my thoughts was hopeless. I watched for the girl at the bus stop every day, imagined her preparing for bed, her sweet breasts emerging into the light as she undressed at night, after they'd been kept so unfairly hidden the whole day. Sin! Sin! I never mentioned *this* sin in confession. Besides, I wasn't really sorry about it. I *enjoyed, more than anything* contemplating those breasts, imagining what it might feel like to touch them. I went to mass and tried to be devout, but mass was so boring, conducted by men who mumbled an incomprehensible language. We were not meant to understand, but rather to bow our heads. And I did. I bowed my head in awe and trembling.

All Catholics, I was taught, must receive communion at least once a year. To miss this ritual was a mortal sin, and a mortal sin, one unconfessed mortal sin, was all it took to send you straight to Hell. Foreverandeverandever. But Mom, I observed, did not go to confession or communion. One day, after Dad and Virginia had left the breakfast table, I asked Mom why she didn't go to communion like everyone else. "It's a mortal sin, you know. I want you to be in Heaven when I get there."

She rearranged the butter dish, setting it on one side of the table, then the other, then clearing it away entirely. I slumped down in my chair. When she returned and saw me still seated, she sat down again. "Come, let's play a game of Parcheesi, shall we?"

"I don't want to play Parcheesi. You have to go to communion. It's the rule. Why don't you go?"

Mom took out the vacuum cleaner and started to vacuum the rug. In all our time in this house, I'd never seen her vacuum the rug.

"Why, Mom? Why don't you go to communion? You'll go to Hell. I don't want you to go to Hell."

My tears finally got to her. She turned off the vacuum cleaner and sat down. She sighed, then waited a long time before she spoke. "Dad, you see, was married before."

"What's that have to do with going to communion?"

"It was a very brief marriage. Just a couple of weeks, in fact, but because of that, we couldn't get married in the church."

"You didn't get married in a church?"

"Not in a Catholic church."

"But in some different church?"

"Yes."

"We were married in the Church of England. But because the Catholic Church doesn't recognize the Church of England, they don't recognize our marriage, and I can no longer take communion."

It was all very confusing. Images of Mom burning in Hell rose before me. Fear and indignation stormed me. Tears welled up. How could this be? "I'll write the pope," I said. "I'll talk to Jesus. They can't send you to Hell." I tried to hug my mother. She patted me on the shoulder and backed away. There were tears in her eyes too. "It's not that bad," she said.

Not that bad? My mother going to Hell, not that bad! What could be worse? The next day at school, I asked Mr. McGrath, if a Catholic is married in some other church and therefore can't go to communion, was that a mortal sin? He knew just where to go in the catechism. He pointed me to the sentence. It was unequivocal. Mom was going to Hell. After she died, I would never see her again.

I walked over to the football field and sat for a long time, alone in the bleachers, watching the daisies grow. I thought about Mom and the torments of Hell. I thought about confession and sin and Adam and Eve and Mom and Dad getting married in some other church and why that was a sin and why she should go to Hell for that, and I couldn't make any sense out of it, but I knew it was true because that was what the priests told me, and they knew. They knew everything.

Chapter 20

The tall man who opens the door leads with a long, scraggly, Rasputinlike beard and a voice that rises, primordial, from a cave somewhere deep in the earth. Toby, one of my two oldest friends in the world, ushers me into his cabinlike retreat in the woods of San Anselmo, outside San Francisco. We walk into his personal library, bookcases from floor to ceiling on all four walls. What amazes me is that he's read every volume. More amazing is that he's thought about what he's read. Most amazing is that he can quote chapter and verse.

I've known Toby since first grade. He's the kind of friend it's good to have when you have a problem, and I have a problem. I tell Toby about the sack of doubt I lug behind me every day.

"You keep the sack well hidden," he says.

"From everyone but myself."

Toby thinks for a moment, his mind like a searchlight scanning hundreds of volumes before he settles on one. "You know what Bertrand Russell said about doubt? 'Fools and fanatics are certain of themselves, but wise people are full of doubts.'"

"I don't think Bertrand Russell was talking about my kind of doubt."

Toby goes to one of his bookcases, down on his knees, second shelf from the bottom. "I'm pretty sure it's in *The Problems of Philosophy*." He snags the quote. "Yes, here it is."

We talk about doubt in Bertrand Russell, doubt in the Bible, doubt in Shakespeare, and Toby's theory that doubt and discovery are kissing cousins. More precisely, Toby talks and I listen. Ask Toby a real question and you get a real answer. Not just a nod or a shrug or a "Wow!" Toby's mind pokes and probes, prances and prognosticates. You can dance around with one topic for an evening.

"Philosophical doubt is one thing." I say, "Personal doubt is different. I'm stuck. The harder I work, the more stuck I become. I'm a car spinning its wheels in mud."

"You said you were trying to find a job. How are you stuck?"

"I search the want ads every day. Most of the jobs bore me. As for the ones I might consider, they'd laugh at my application. I'm all over the map."

Toby scratches his beard. "You say you're looking in the want ads?"

"That's where you look for a job."

Toby points to his head. "First, you have to create it up here. Have you imagined the job you want?"

I shake my head. "I don't write the want ads. I read them."

"Remember the Rumi story about the drunk on the street searching for his house key?" Toby asks.

I shake my head. "Tell me."

"This guy is out in the street, under a street lamp, searching for his key. He hunts for hours, but he can't find the key. A friend asks. 'Are you sure you lost it out here?'

"'I lost it in the house.'

"'So why are you searching in the street?'

"'Because I can see better, here under the light.'"

I laugh. Toby is quiet. Then I confess, "I don't really get it."

"Looking for a job in the want ads is like the drunk searching for his key in the street," Toby says. "It may be easier to search the want ads, but you won't find what you're looking for there. That's not where you lost it."

"I'm not sure I ever had it."

"What you're looking for is inside. In here." Toby points to his head, and then his heart. "The key is inside. You have to tap in to the power of your imagination. If you can imagine it, you may be able to create it."

I frown. Ask a philosopher a question and you get a philosopher's answer. I want something plain and simple. Something I can understand. Something actionable, not a reading from the Oracle at Delphi.

"Thanks, Toby." My sarcasm oozes across the table. "So what do I do now? Consult my chart?" Toby is an astrologer, too.

"You could," he says. "There are many roads. For a start, get rid of the want ads. Look inside."

Back at home, I think about our conversation. The more I ponder, the more angry I become. Who is Toby, to be telling me I need to "look inside"? I'm about to write him a letter when I stop to ponder again. Could there be any truth in what he says?

I grab my journal and start scribbling, fast, whatever comes to mind. Fifteen pages later, I read what I've written. The word "job" doesn't appear once. I look at my watch. Almost 2:00 a.m. I light a candle. It flickers across the page, whispering to me, one word over and over: "Truth." Okay, I'll meditate on the idea of truth. I ask my higher self to reveal the truth to me, and promise that I will follow it, no matter what. When I finish, I write a short note to Toby.

Dear Toby,

First, my apology. I was not ready to hear what you said at dinner. I was defensive. I'm slow but now I recognize what you were trying to tell me. It's not just a job. I'm searching for something deeper. Who am I? What am I really all about—beyond job and role? Who gets to decide this? And another fundamental question: Am I worth it? How do I shake my self-doubt and get off this crooked path to nowhere? Maybe you and Rumi told me the story I needed to hear. I'm no longer searching out in the street. The key is inside the house. Somewhere. Where?

With deep appreciation and love,
Peter

Mark Twain wrote, "There are two important dates in any life: the date you were born and the date you discover why you were born." I'm ready for that second date. I've been all over the map, spinning in circles, trying on hats, discarding each of them once I proved I could wear it. The problem is not the hat, but the head beneath the hat.

Once I begin talking about my struggle, teachers in the guise of friends, lovers, therapists, strangers, dreams, and books drop from the sky. I follow guidance from *What Color Is Your Parachute*, a career guidebook by Richard Bolles. I read every word and complete every exercise. I begin a process of identifying beliefs and values, visions for myself, skills I have and skills I lack. I am no longer thinking job. I am thinking career, thinking lifestyle, thinking identity. Thinking what I care about, how I want to spend my life. I interview people in different careers; I shadow people who are working in ways that sound interesting to me; I dream dreams, follow hunches, and search under mattresses. Who knows where buried treasure lies?

I hear a symphony orchestra conductor tell a story about how at age nine, after his first-ever symphony concert, he approached the conductor: "When I grow up, I want to do what you're doing. How do I become a conductor?" He followed the conductor's advice and never looked back. Discovering one's purpose at such a young age would be sweet, but that path was not mine. I stumbled about lost in the desert for years. Messy as it is, I come to believe that there is a wisdom that may be found only in the search.

After months of exploration, I narrow my search to the field of conflict resolution. I participate in workshops, study mediation, read everything I can find, and talk with as many practitioners as possible. Following a day of informational interviews in San Francisco, I am walking north on Ninth Street toward Mission to catch the bus home when I pass a storefront window, filled with a pyramid of small yellow books, *How to Make Meetings Work*, by Michael Doyle and David Straus. What a bizarre subject to write a book about,

I think, then walk on. The image of the little yellow books haunts me. On the bus ride home, when I close my eyes, I see the pyramid of books again and again. My brain tingles. What is this all about?

A week later, I fly back to Washington, DC, to take a class in mediation. While back in Washington, I tell my instructor that I'm interested in conflict resolution, or even more, conflict prevention, if there is any such thing. He smiles. "Where did you say you live?"

"Near San Francisco."

"Visit Interaction Associates. It's a small consulting company, right in your backyard. They're doing the best conflict-prevention work in the country," he advises.

Back in San Francisco, I head for the address I've found for Interaction Associates. Once there, I am immediately thrust into the twilight zone. I stand in front of the same storefront window, with the same pyramid of yellow books that had grabbed my attention a week earlier.

I think back to the red-winged blackbird and to Toby's Rumi story. Were these seemingly random events leading me here? When the universe bonks you on the head, it's wise to listen. I brush back my hair in awkward deference to the moment, then step over the threshold to find out who and what is behind these yellow books. I approach the receptionist and recognize her accent as German. When I respond in German, she smiles. *"Wo haben Sie so gut Deutsch gelernt?"* (Where did you learn to speak such good German?)

I tell her about my air force time in Germany. Normally I'd stop there and we'd go on with our business. But this is no normal time. I tell Gabrielle the story of hiring Frau

Klinke in Germany, how Sally sewed cotton balls on the hairnet and Frau Klinke mediated our frequent squabbles. "I've wanted to learn more about facilitation and mediation ever since."

Gabrielle smiles. "You came to the right place."

I look her right in the eye. "I was sent here."

"Sent here! By whom?"

One word comes to mind. "A prophet." It sounds weird, but…

"A prophet?" Gabrielle looks dubious.

I'm quick to clarify. I tell her the story of how I've been haunted ever since I saw the little yellow books in the window, and then my prophetic meeting in Washington. "It was like a voice telling me I had to come back here. I had to pay attention. There are some connections out there, beyond the normal, I mean." I back off the topic, not wanting to sound to woo-woo.

Gabrielle nods knowingly. "You need a tour of the office." She shows me photos, tells me a lot about David and Michael, cofounders of the company, and explains some of the projects they're involved in. I soak it up. The more she tells me, the more my heart sings. I try not to drool. I pick up brochures, sign up for an introductory seminar, buy and devour the little yellow book.

Before I leave, Gabrielle gives me one last gift. "When David gets back in town, I'll tell him about your visit. You two would enjoy each other."

Three weeks later and two hours into the introductory seminar, my initial instincts are confirmed. This is about so much more than meetings. It is about collaboration, about inspiration, about helping people to work effectively together to achieve their most noble aspirations. My head spins. My heart goes pitter-patter. This is meaningful work. I can do this work. I want to do this work. I will do this work.

I volunteer for facilitation work with any and every organization that is interested. The work speaks to me. Could this be the key? I write David Straus, president of Interaction Associates. A week later, there's a message on my answering machine. "Gabrielle told me about your visit. Let's talk."

I sit with David in his office. It is like falling in love or watching your favorite chestnut grow into a strong tree. My doubting demons scamper to the hills.

"Collaborative planning is ready to take off," David tells me. "Facilitation is the key. We have a social technology that works." I join IA just in time to participate in a project to design and facilitate a multistakeholder process for a new cultural and commercial center, what will become the Yerba Buena Center, in San Francisco's South of Market district. The project languishes while builders grow old, costs double, and the land lies fallow. Federal and state agencies have been suing each other for years. Finally they hire Interaction Associates (IA) to help.

I am thrilled to be part of IA. We start to grow the company. I become a full partner. I think back to the pyramid of little yellow books. How amazing life can be when I open my heart and allow life in. Follow the heart. What better guide is there for life?

Finding my career with Interaction Associates is a huge step forward. It gives me a sense of grounding and purpose in life, what I'd hoped religion might do, what religion had promised but never delivered for me. The sense of mission and the work at Interaction Associates buoys me for several years, long enough that for some time, I believe my troubles are over. But the demons don't give up easily. The doubts wait for their moment. I still try too hard to please everyone—my bosses, my clients, my assistants. Doubt drips through me like water seeping in through an old roof that has been patched when it needs to be replaced. With each passing storm, the leakage grows worse.

First it is doubt about myself. Am I good enough?

Then it is doubt about the work itself. Are we smoke and mirrors? Are we doing anything real, anything lasting?

And finally, doubt about life itself. Is there any meaning? No matter how satisfying or successful the work is, or I am, career and work alone can never solve the fundamental problem. A new roof won't fix a faulty foundation.

I remember so clearly that first day on the job with Interaction Associates, the Yerba Buena planning conference with David. David is facilitating a huge meeting in which artists and leaders from every arts organization for miles around are present, each lobbying for the kind of cultural center they envision. I am to be David's gopher, responsible for room setup, which involves cutting hundreds of sheets of butcher paper to hang on the walls, so participants' comments can be recorded in view of everyone. I am meticulously decked out in my new facilitation uniform: polished shoes, new haircut, Irish Donegal wool jacket, and my favorite tie from the Museum of Modern Art in New York. My tie is decorated with images of Vincent Van Gogh's painting of the wicker chair in the corner of his bedroom in the asylum at Arles. Could there be a more appropriate tie to wear before a group of artists?

Ten minutes before the meeting start time. Everything is ready. I review my room setup. Adequate butcher paper in neat stacks across the walls, check. Microphones in place and operating, check. Electronic voting systems on every chair, check. Facilitators and recorders briefed and in place, check. I give myself an A. David is conferring with the meeting principles. I duck into the men's room for a last look in the mirror to ensure that every hair is in place. A shock wave bounces back at me from the mirror. Where my Van Gogh tie should be, a pathetic three-inch stub dangles. A pebble where I need a boulder. While cutting the butcher paper, I have somehow sliced off the bottom two-thirds of my tie.

The meeting starts in five minutes. I have to go. I fashion Vincent's remains into a crude bow tie, then enter stage right for Act 1, Scene 1 of my new career. David is too busy to notice.

Chapter 21

It was 1956. Ike's million-dollar smile shone over us, the icon of the era. Our lawns were green. Milk was still delivered daily to the home. There was wistfulness in the air when Gogi Grant crooned "The Wayward Wind," but the loudest sound of the year was the crack of Mickey Mantle's bat. There were eight teams in each major league. Life was manageable—pre-drugs, pre-Viet Nam, pre-Watergate, no assassinations since William McKinley—and who was he, anyway?

After two years of Catholic school, I'd transferred to a small, private boys' school outside of Washington, a school known as a national tennis powerhouse. Once I left the crucifix and the confessional behind, I quickly recognized that I was not going to wake up on Good Friday morning with the blood of the stigmata on my hands and feet. But if I was not destined to be a saint or a priest, then who was I? In my new school, I reverted to nameless-faceless. I fell back on my basic approach to anything, trying to please. The warts of self-doubt infested my body and polluted my mind.

I assessed the culture of this new school and made up two rules for myself: be cool and win your tennis matches. It would take time to watch and learn how to be cool, but the rules for winning at tennis were clear enough. This school expected to win and rewarded those who did. I fantasized myself as a world champion, parading around Wimbledon holding the silver cup over my head. I was far from world class, but after a few years, I'd rise to number one on the varsity team, where I learned that when you are number one in anything, others aim to get you.

Tim and I were in the locker room dressing for our challenge tennis match that would determine if I'd stay at number one or if he'd replace me. Tim's wallet dropped on the floor. A small, square tinfoil package fell out. He picked it up, laughed, held it out to me like a trophy. "Let's get this match over quickly. I've got a date tonight with Nancy Hartinger. I'll need this." He rubbed the package between his thumb and forefinger. "You need one? I've got extras."

Tim was a friendly guy, a good friend, even if he was my archrival on the tennis team.

"I have my own," I said. Truth was, I'd stolen furtive glances at them, hanging neatly in their blue and tan shiny wrapping, out of reach but not out of view, lined up behind the clerk in the drug store, there for the asking by bigger, braver boys than I. I'd never dared ask. Nor had I ever needed one.

I slipped into white tennis shorts and my good luck Izod shirt. All the big-time players wore Izod. I imagined that if I dressed like Tony Trabert, I'd play like Tony Trabert. Something missing in that logic, but it sold a lot of shirts.

The afternoon sun beat down on the hard clay court. Tim won the first set. He was ahead five to four in the second. One game away from victory, stealing my number one spot from me. I saw him check his watch, thinking about his date, no doubt. If I could win this next game, then take the set, he'd get distracted, lose his focus. The school buses coughed and sputtered up the hill, taking the younger kids home. Their day was done. Mine was reaching its climax. My legs wobbled. I twirled the racket handle in my hand, gripped the dark patches where sweat had penetrated the leather. *Bear down, Peter. This is it.*

I served, came to net. The ball zinged back and forth. Wop. Wop. Tim's lob was over my head. I ran back for it but couldn't quite reach it. "Out." I heard the word, but almost as if from some other voice. But there was no other voice.

"What?" Tim, from across the net. "It couldn't have been out."

"Your lob was half an inch out."

Tim banged his racket against the net. "Impossible."

"It was out."

Later that evening, after I'd listened to Elvis sing "Heartbreak Hotel" ten times in a row, and crawled into bed, the ball bounced again and again in my mind. Every bounce echoed the same hollow word, "out…out…out." And Tim, coming to the net over and over, his mouth agape, shaking his head, waving his racket, "Impossible! Impossible!" He repeated overandoverandover, like some TV ad, repeated it ad nauseam. Then the spank of his racket against the tape at the top of the net, how he stood there while I returned to the base line for the next point. After the match, in the locker room, he wouldn't speak to me. I was still number one, but I was not cool.

The next day, I passed Tim in the hallway. "Hey, how

was your date? Did you need the rubbers?" Even to me, my voice sounded phony. He turned away without response. That night, I dreamed about the match. I decided to confess, then forfeit the challenge to him. I approached him after lunch, "Tim, I want to"—the intended words clogged in my throat—"play again sometime. Maybe next week. It was so close."

His cold green eyes pierced my sunny exterior. Without tennis I was nothing. Tim had his rubbers.

There was tennis and there was cool. The effort to be cool started each morning on the bus to school. The ride was a journey from a lonely world where I knew what to expect into a lonely world where I had no idea what to expect. I boarded early and sat in the same seat every day, two-thirds of the way back, on the left, by the window. I was the first to board the bus, so it was fine to be alone, but later, as the bus filled, my fears rumbled about like bumper cars inside my brain. Would anyone sit next to me? Who would notice that I was alone? What would they think? Stressing about who might sit next to me was even less cool than sitting alone, which was not at all cool in the first place. The only thing even remotely cool about my bus ride was that I had learned the unspoken rule never to let on that you cared about anything.

George was the first in my class after me to board. George was cool. As we approached his stop, my palms began to sweat. The bus slowed. I peered out the window to see if he was there. He was. I tuned in to the hiss of the breaks and the squeak of the opening door, checked out the thunk of footsteps on the bus steps, searching for any sign from George as he stumbled toward me, the only thing in the world that mattered: would George sit next to me? I buried my head in my book, pretending to be cramming for the second-period geometry quiz, desperate to be cool, never to let on that I cared or even noticed. If he sat next to me—18 percent of the time, according to my records—I smiled inside like a field of sunflowers, then acknowledged his presence with a nonchalant mumble, "Uh, yeah." If he sat somewhere else, I buried my head even deeper in geometry as my eyes blinked back the rejection that swirled inside me. Depending on George, I was king of the mountain or whale shit on the bottom of the sea.

When we arrived at school, if George had passed me by, I now had to worry about anybody looking in the window of the bus and seeing me sitting there, all alone. Super uncool. I slinked down as low as I could, buried my head as low as I could, and pulled up my jacket, praying for anonymity as I shuffled off the bus, the day already lost.

It might have been easier to accept George's choice not to sit with me if I'd had a girlfriend, but as soon as I felt some attraction to a girl, I got too serious and clammed up. Then, in the spring, Shelley, a cute, bubbly blonde, picked me out of the crowd and inexplicably became my shadow. I never understood it. She was one of the most popular girls, far above my reach, but relishing my good fortune, I went with it. I spent evenings at her house, watching TV and sucking Pez candies. I dreamed of kissing her and thought she wanted to kiss me, but doubt loomed like an electric fence in the space between her lips and mine. Night after night, I brimmed with steely resolve, but when the moment arrived, I melted. Walking home, I lectured myself, *Finked out again, loser.*

One evening we went out bowling. I obsessed about the kiss. When? And where? And how? I had watched other boys, many of them so casual, the way they tossed their arms around a girl's shoulder and pulled her in close. I had studied the cool guys at parties, how they curled up with their girls on the couch and made out for hours, lips locked together, grinding on like a slow-motion movie with a sound track of wistful moans. Once in the car John had necked with Pam all the way from River Road out to Glen Echo while my date and I huddled self-consciously in the back seat next to them, squished, silent, and embarrassed, flush against the door.

Shelley and I bowled one game, then another. After each ball, she sidled over and sat as close on the bench to me as possible. Her eyes begged. *How about it? How about now? Right here at Randy's Bowling, lane number nine. Why not?* I gazed at her and my hand inched across the bench toward her…but I was up and collecting my next ball, locked in to bowling while thinking only of kissing. By the third game Shelley had switched to the bench across from me. She stared at her watch, the Coke machine, her shoes. She crossed and uncrossed her legs, went to the bathroom, yawned, went to the bathroom again. So ready was she. So still thinking and plotting was I. Maybe as we walked out the door, I'd take her hand, then out in the street. No, that's not cool. Maybe at the bus stop. No, that's not right either.

Back at her place, when the bowling was finished and still no kiss, we climbed the concrete steps to her house. We stopped at the landing. Her lips glistened under the porch light. I made two fists, pumped and committed. Now. It must be now, or I'm a useless wimp forever.

Standing before her front door, I slipped my arm around her tiny waist. Her body slid toward me. No resistance. She put her arms around my neck, gazed, expectantly, radiantly even, at me. Her lips parted ever so slightly. She had the prettiest eyes in the world, soft, blue, and luminous. Her lips were moist, like melted butter. Ready. I sensed the gentle pressure of her thighs against mine, her small breasts, her hands now gently massaging my neck, our lips closer, ever closer. Three inches, two, one.

And then, like a cannon in the night, it boomed, the fart of the century, echoing off buildings up and down the street, sending shock waves throughout dear little Shelley, sending a flash of flushed humiliation that zapped my red, red face. In less time than you could say "P-yu," I had disappeared. Out of there. Into the night. Wimp forever.

I laugh about it now. At the time, not funny.

*

At school, every senior had to give a speech—ten to twelve minutes—to qualify for graduation. All speeches were delivered to the entire high school student body. The subject, once approved by the faculty advisor, was optional, but there were mandatory guidelines. Pity the fellow who did not follow them.

1. Outline your speech first, including one main point and two to three sub-points.
2. Practice your speech, exactly as you plan to deliver it. The tone should be serious, controlled, and calm.

3. On speech day, look sharp, get a haircut, wear your best, cleanest, smartest clothes.

4. Walk briskly up to the podium, project an image of confidence and knowledge.

5. Address your talk to "Mr. Banfield, Faculty, and Students."

6. The classic: Tell 'em what you're going to tell 'em; tell 'em; then tell 'em what you told 'em.

To graduate, you had to pass. To pass, you had to follow the rules. We all wanted to graduate. We all followed the rules

As my day to speak approached, I was submerged, as usual, in doubt. I had spent the summer before my senior year working on a cattle ranch in Colorado and decided to speak about that experience. The topic was approved, but as the date approached, I couldn't fit the mystery of the experience into the required format, which worked fine for Washington lawyers, but not so well for Colorado cowboys. I wrote out my conventional speech about the dying industry of the small cattle ranch and the looming reality of agribusiness, nothing about camping alone under the stars, nothing about the freedom I felt riding with real cowboys on the range, and nothing about how I guzzled a few cold Coors beers at the end of the day. My speech was clear, correct, and dull. All I had to do was dress for the occasion, walk up the steps to the podium, and read. Not brilliant, but it would pass.

I dressed in my best tweed jacket, fresh blue shirt and tie, but in a last-minute impulse, I toted a small bag with props for a different kind of speech that had been bubbling inside me. I sat in the large assembly hall, fidgeting and wondering. Minutes before my turn to speak, I was still undecided. A voice inside whispered, "Do it." It was a voice I'd heard often, and ignored consistently. This time—I don't know why; maybe my doubting demons were asleep—was different. I ducked out of the assembly room for a quick clothes change. When my name was called, I galloped in through the double doors and leapt on to the stage dressed in cowboy boots, Levis, a mud-spattered wrangler's shirt, and cowboy hat. Ignoring the mandatory "Mr. Banfield, Faculty, and Students," I opened with a wave of my cowboy hat and a whoop that echoed off the rafters: "Howdy, Pardner!"

Seventy-five percent of the students had been barely awake since the first speech. There was a shuffling of feet, heads upright for the first time, blasé freshmen whispering to their neighbors, "Isn't he that quiet tennis-player guy?"

"Yeah, it's me," I wanted to yell. "The real me, not the me you know." I was instantly back on the ranch, where I could smell the hay and the fresh manure and the clear mountain air. I told raunchy ranch stories—about slicing off a bull's balls and cooking them over the campfire, "Rocky Mountain oysters," we called 'em. Before we ate them. I told them how I backed the tractor so far into the dump that the whole trailer fell in; how one night under the stars taught me more about my soul than all the hours I'd spent in church; and how my carefully learned rules of grammar from Mr. Dixon's English class didn't make one whit of difference on the ranch. I was not aware of time, barely aware that I was giving a speech. And when I was finished, wiped out and covered with sweat, instead of my carefully worded "and in conclusion" sentence, I belched and laughed, "Well,

I guess it's time for a Coors," and I popped open a can, in front of Mr. Banfield, the faculty, and the students. The audience gave me a standing ovation that was longer than the speech, with foot stomping and cheers and yells. It was the highlight of my high-school career.

As we filed out of assembly, George tapped me on the shoulder. "You know you broke every one of the speech rules."

"You heard the applause," I retorted in uncharacteristic boldness. "They can't flunk me."

"Sure they can."

But they didn't.

I returned to class, flushed with success. Of course, by the end of the day, everyone had forgotten my speech and we were back to school as usual.

On the bus, George sat on the opposite isle, two rows behind me. I was still not cool.

Chapter 22

Shortly after I am hired at Interaction Associates, I start volunteer work on a crisis-counseling and child-abuse telephone hotline. Once or twice a year, the hotline hosts a disco party. I go alone. Fifty or so people mill around as I arrive, others mix it up at tables over cheap wine and rubber chicken. Small groups stand around drinking, some already dancing to music of the Bee Gees' "Too Much Heaven." Crepe paper streamers hang from the ceiling. Low lights and a rotating disco mirror ball set the tone.

I head for the bar. Jim and I have worked together as trainers for new volunteers. He watches the spinning mirror light. "It looks like a night for love."

I do a double take. "What do you mean?"

"I don't know," he shrugs. "Just a feeling."

"I wish." Despite all the personal-growth work I've done, I've never been close to finding a life partner. Over the years, I've developed a belief about myself: I am a bachelor, a seeker not a finder, a cave dweller, someone who comes and goes on the outskirts of society. Is this story true? Is it just the story I tell myself? Is that the fundamental truth, the story we tell ourselves? Or is there more?

"Don't wish," Jim says. "Make it happen."

"Just like that," I tease. Jim is married with family. Eight children.

"Right," he says.

After several hours, no love in sight for me, I'm ready to leave. Other than with Jim, the conversation has been desultory, the food forgettable: Gallo wine, rubber chicken, heaps of French fries, like so many other parties, not what I had hoped for.

I'm half out the door when two women dancing together catch my attention. One of them looks ordinary, but the other is a pixie, dancing in slow, undulating rhythms, her skirt swaying like gentle waves at the beach. My eyes lock. She moves, but not to the music of this party. She is following a different beat, music that seems to come from within. She bends in a slow, sensuous motion, her body swaying gently, so natural she is, easy, unaware of her own grace rippling in the wind.

I finish my wine, try to remember where I parked my car, toss an imaginary good-bye kiss to the pixie. I'm just about out the door when the music turns up-tempo. I look to see if she is still on the dance floor. She is. I watch as she tosses her shoes to the side, then throws her body into the dance with abandon, swinging her arms from side to side, reaching out as if she's embracing the whole world, spinning as if she *is* the whole world, and maybe she is. She kicks back her heels, swooping now and diving, soaring, climbing, leaping, delighting herself, delighting me, her hair wild in its up-spring, beads of sweat forming on her forehead, dripping down her cheeks until she brushes the sweat aside in tiny gestures that send me shooting into space like a rocket from NASA. I watch mesmerized as she dances, a dance of unselfconscious seduction, a dance of hope and mystery. I come alive, drift into reverie, imagine myself lying with her, on a beach far away, no one else for miles, our bodies entwined, waves breaking over us, salty water washing our lips, waves of passion and tenderness, toes playing in the sand, sun baking our backs, legs braided together, arms wrapped around each other, our hands exploring up and down and in and out, along the long beaches of our bodies, reaching in to the inlets and the gullies, separate no more.

I close my eyes. A minute, an hour. Who knows? Who cares?

When I open my eyes and return to the party, she is gone.

I scour the room. Was she a mirage? The wild imagination of a lonely…? "NO!" *She was here. She is real.* I search. *Where is she? Who is she?* "Jim, did you see…do you know?" He shakes his head. Did anyone see? I dash to the door and stare into the darkness. At first, nothing. Then I see two figures. The pixie is walking across the parking lot, shoes in hand. A man walks a few feet in front of her.

Hesitation is betrayal. I bolt out the door, reaching her as she is about to get in the car. I have no idea what I am going to say. Something. Anything. "Excuse me. I couldn't help…Can we? Could we?"

She looks at me, sweat still streaming down her cheek. "One dance?"

Her eyes widen in arched surprise. She glances at the driver. He shrugs, gets in the car. I wait. I watch her chest rise and fall, still panting from the dance. The parking lot lights cast a yellow glow. "One dance?" I repeat.

She smiles and nods. "One dance."

My heart somersaults.

We walk back inside. Her face and hair are covered in sweat. Her eyes sparkle. We dance. I am half in the room and half still out on that beach. When the music stops, she smiles again and says, "That was fun. Would you like to go out dancing again sometime?"

I nod. She jots down a phone number on a scrap of paper. "I'm Wendy."

She disappears. Back into the night.

Chapter 23

"How was school today?" Mom hunched forward over the dining room table and squinted at Virginia and me with her left, the "good" eye. Her watery right eye drooped like a flag on a still day, the result of a botched surgery to remove a cataract. Our family huddled behind closed, heavy venetian blinds that shielded us from outside eyes. Mom supported her head in her right hand, as if it was a heavy rock she was condemned to hold.

"Fine," Virginia said.

"Fine," I said. My day had been as unfine as a day could be, but I was not about to say that. I was counting the days, marking time until I graduated from high school, working on my own ways to close myself off from the outside world.

"I'm sorry about the chicken lush," Mom passed the plates around the table. "Something went wrong. I don't know what."

It was the eighteenth Tuesday in a row we'd had chicken lush. On Thursdays we had reheated chicken lush.

Mom and Dad, Virginia, and I gathered around the dining room table, like a Norman Rockwell painting. We lived in a neighborhood of brick colonial homes, green lawns, chipmunks, and golfers, Chevy Chase, Maryland, near the border with Washington, DC. Our street was clean, orderly, and quiet, crocuses in small patches on both sides of front doors. Kitty corner, across the street, was the stately brick Mormon Church. Young Mormon boys in white shirts and narrow, dark ties, and girls in printed calf-length dresses descended on us, practicing for their missions. On the outside, everything was in order, everything right with America, our neighborhood, and our lives. Inside, we were like mummies in a museum that had closed for the winter.

Mom puckered her face like she'd gulped a glass of sour milk. "I put a tablespoon of salt in, when the recipe calls for a teaspoon." She shook her head, then buried it deeper in her hand. "I'm such a dunce. Here, give it to me. I'll heat up some Campbell's soup."

Dad tapped a teaspoon on the table and hummed, "Sugar in the morning, sugar in the evening, sugar at supper time, be my little sugar, and love me all the time." Dad was the happiest man in the world. He smiled, he walked the dog, he played golf. It was enough. "Don't tell 'em," he smiled.

Mom's voice quivered. "Don't eat it. It's inedible."

Dad took a bite. "It's fine and dandy."

"When you were born"—Mom looked at Virginia—"I didn't know how to boil an egg. And now look at me. I can't follow a recipe. A first-class dunce, that's what I am. I'll make some mushroom soup."

Virginia slumped in her chair. "I don't like mushroom soup."

"I'll be right back." Mom sloughed into the kitchen. I watched her staring into the soup, as if she could see her whole life in that can, and she couldn't figure out how she got there or what it meant, because she was brought up to be a society girl, and yet here she was, rattling around inside a can of soup with a husband who barely noticed her.

Her hand shook as she placed the soup bowls on the table. She tried to clear Dad's plate, but he held it tight. She flopped down at her place. Our silence was scratched only by the slurping of soup. Dad called Geordie, our Sealyham terrier, and handed him a piece of the chicken lush.

"Otie, don't feed Geordie from the table." Mom shook her head. "I've told you that a thousand times."

Dad hummed another bar of "Sugar in the Morning" and gave Geordie more chicken lush. A tear started down Mom's cheek. The tear balanced precariously on her chin for a moment, then fell, ka-plop, into the mushroom soup and disappeared.

Mom peered into the bowl. "Mayma had a story she liked to tell. A lady whose nose often dripped was giving a dinner party. She told her butler that if her nose dripped during dinner, he was to tap her on the shoulder and say, 'Mr. Jones is at the door,' and she would understand what that meant. During dinner, the butler tapped the lady on the shoulder several times, but she was too engrossed in conversation to stop. Each time the butler tapped, the lady said, 'Not now, James.' After several attempts, the butler tapped her on the shoulder one last time. 'Mr. Jones was at the door, but he's in the soup now.'" Mom paused, scanned the table to assess our reactions. "Isn't that a delightful story?"

"Can we be excused?" Virginia asked.

Dad lit his pipe, then pushed back from the table. As always, he was dressed in sport coat and tie. With his British accent, he was a cross between the Kodak baby and the

Duke of Edinburgh. While Mom's story dissolved along with her tears in the soup, Dad's smile spread across the table like maple syrup. "Beautiful, the way that ball rolled across the tenth green yesterday, like it knew exactly where to go."

While Dad blissed his way through the day, Mom fretted about the food and the locks on the front door and whether the cleaning lady was stealing her jewelry and whether her clothes matched and were they clean and pressed and would the money last.

Mom and Dad opted for peace over passion, golf over glitter. Their world, once painted with glamor, had dulled to gray. They spent most of the day in the den, a six-by-nine dark box of a room, with two ragged, overstuffed chairs, a tiny TV, and heavy blinds drawn closed, even on sunny days. A built-in bookshelf was filled with dust and books, from decades past. The silence was broken only by the crackle of turning pages from the *Washington Post* and the whispers of TV golf commentators.

Mom's bank account was sufficient to sustain a comfortable lifestyle. After she and Dad returned to the United States from England, Dad never worked again. He played golf, or as Mom phrased it, he "brought home the bacon," her way of helping Dad believe that he was contributing financially, and helping herself believe that her husband was contributing in some ill-defined way. On a good day, the bacon from small bets on the golf course added up to ten dollars. Occasionally Dad and I played golf together, like he was taking me to the office. One time we were in a foursome with Joe Swanson, a retired dentist and an erratic golfer. After one of his drives, Dr. Swanson yelled "fore" as his ball caromed off the tee at ninety degrees, smacking Dad right in the mouth.

The dentist rushed over, clad in worry. "Let me see in your mouth," he insisted. Moments later, with a deep sigh of relief, he announced, "Well, at least you didn't lose any teeth." Whereupon Dad reached down and picked up four bright white teeth sprouting like daisies in the grass. Dad smiled, as always. There was a huge gap in the lower floor of his smile for months after this. Then one day the gap was magically filled with four shiny new teeth. "I saw Dr. Swanson today," was all Dad said.

Since we moved to Chevy Chase, Mom and Dad had rarely traveled more than the two miles required to go to the grocery store or the golf course. Dad walked the dog twice a day. Other than golf, his greatest pleasure was smoking his pipe, four or five times a day, every day of his life, until an overzealous doctor put the fear of god into him. "The smoking is killing you." The day that Dad discarded his pipe collection was the day he began a descent down a slide that had no ascent.

A lot of the time Mom and Dad seemed barely to notice one another. Mom, Dad, and I, plus Geordie, were out for a walk one day. Dad always walked a few steps ahead, whistling and twirling his walking stick like a drum major. On the golf course, they all called him "The Commander," because he was, in fact, a retired commander in the British navy, but he was the most uncommanderlike person. When he got his front bridge and his smile back, he was once again seemingly irresistible to women. Mazie Thurston, our neighbor from four doors down, spotted us from a block away and headed over.

"Hello, Mazie, how nice to see you." Mom tossed a sideways grimace, then stared down the road at a chipmunk who was debating his options for which tree to climb.

"Charles"—Mazie moved a step closer to Dad—"your crocuses are lovely. What kind of bulbs do you use?"

"I got them at the Giant," Dad answered, as if Mazie were, at that very moment, off to buy bulbs.

Mazie leaned in like an admiring teenybopper at the foot of her favorite rock star. "Are you fertilizing?"

"Yes, he fertilizes," Mom said. "Well, Mazie, we hate to run, but you know . . . Come on, Charles. We have to get back."

But Dad was deep into the crocus patch with Mazie. "I water them and watch them grow," he said.

"Mine are hopeless," Mazie said.

"I'm leaving," Mom said.

Geordie raised his leg. I shoved my hands in my pockets. Mom, Geordie, and I departed. Just before we turned at the end of the block, Mom looked back down the road. Dad and Mazie were still lost in the crocus patch.

When we got home, Mom double locked the front door.

"How will Dad get in?" I asked.

"He'll figure it out."

A half-hour later, Dad entered through the back door, still humming "Sugar in the Morning." He never mentioned the double-locked front door, apparently never noticed Mom's glower. He was still humming "Sugar in the Morning." "Mazie has a new kind of fall crocus bulb," he announced. "Purple flowers, like lilacs. She's going to give me some."

Mom stood over the kitchen sink, shaking. She glanced at me, hands raised in resignation. "We may as well have something to eat." In the dining room, Mazie floated invisibly above the table, dangling crocuses from her charm bracelet.

I sat silent at the table. I loved my parents, with a kind of benign love. But I so didn't want to be like them. Mom, Dad, Virginia, and I moved about the house like airplanes circling an airport, eyeing each other, measuring and preserving our distance. We avoided accidents. And we avoided connection. Near contact happened, but rarely. The overarching principle of our family was "Never speak what can be left unspoken." The unsaid circled around our heads, like an airplane requesting permission to land, unrecognized by the control tower. When I spent time at home, I thought I was going to suffocate. How could it be that I had everything I needed, yet felt like I was lacking the most important things of all. I tried my hardest to fit in, but there was no place to land. There was something off-center about us, about me. I didn't know what to call it. Something off.

*

Every family develops its own unique rituals. One of the defining traditions in our house occurred around gift giving at Christmas. Traditionally, presents, of course, are displayed at the base of the Christmas tree, but we'd shunned the tree in favor of chairs in the living room. Each member of the family was assigned a chair. The four of us, plus Geordie, move from chair to chair, each of us opening a present in turn until all the presents were gone, paper and ribbon covering the floor and we'd used up all our oohs and ahs and ways to say thank you. The last time we conducted this Christmas ritual was the year that Dad tried to open everyone else's presents.

"No, Dad. Those are Mom's presents. Yours are over here," Virginia coaxed him gently across the room to his chair.

Dad ignored the injunction. He picked up another present from the nearest chair. Dementia rattled its keys like an angry jailer. After the gift opening, Dad sat in the den, a vacant stare occupying the space that was once his winning smile. Soon, he could no longer feed himself, then no longer speak and no longer recognize anyone. Here was the dashing British Navy pilot. Here was "Sugar in the Morning." Here, this empty shell.

Mom hired live-in help so he could stay at home, but time was running out. He lay in bed all day. It had been eighteen months since he had responded to anything or anyone. A young, attractive nurse substituted one day for the regular caretaker. When the new nurse danced into his room, Dad rose up from his pillow, sat up in bed in a way he hadn't in years. His eyes tracked her across the room. Eyes left, eyes right, following her every move. His eyes widened. His jaw dropped. She bent over the chair to straighten the pillow. He leaned forward, lowering his head for a better angle. She picked up his shoes. He stretched further forward. For one miraculous moment, he was a teenager again, a rocket bursting in the sky on the Fourth of July, hope and desire bundled together for one last, glorious surge. I watched in amazement, half expecting this diapered man with missing teeth who hadn't spoken in years to jump out of bed and leap across the room and take her hand, then to caress the tender mountains and valleys of this angel. And I wished, oh, how I wished, that he could.

She left. Dad slumped back down.

Mom stood in the doorway and took it all in. Not a word was spoken

Near the end, we set up a hospital bed in the living room. We gathered around. The last smile had long since withered. No more sugar in the morning. The breathing slowed. We watched and waited. *Get some juice. Put ice on his lips.* Death is so often portrayed as startling and dramatic, but it is often more a slow, tedious retreat. And then it's over.

The undertakers arrived. I watched them move the body to the stretcher and wheel him out. "Goodbye, Dad." I didn't know what else to say. Mom was already at the breakfast table, still in her robe. I stood at the window and watched the hearse turning out of the driveway. "He's gone," I said to no one in particular.

"The coffee is weak," Mom said. "I don't understand why. Would you like some eggs?" Once Mom, Virginia, and I were seated, Mom released her report, "I hear it's going to be a high of eighty today. Do you have plans?"

"We need to make arrangements," I said.

"Oh, thanks. I don't need anything. Dinner is all set."

She must not have heard. "Arrangements…for Dad," I explained.

"I have a Smithfield ham in the fridge," she said. "They're delicious. You like ham. We can have some green beans too. You like beans, don't you?"

"Virginia and I had talked about a memorial service. You want a memorial service, don't you?"

"More coffee, anyone? Tea?" Forty-five minutes later the conversation has shifted to the O. J. trial. Mom suddenly went quiet. "I have this song going around in my head. 'Thanks for the Memories.' I don't know why that song." My eyes popped. "It's an old song," she continued. "Long before your time, either of you."

Breakfast wound down. I leaned forward. "Mom, we have to make plans."

"I told you I have a Smithfield ham all ready for dinner."

"For Dad. The body. We have to—"

"Stop it!" Her butterfly voice sounded more like a referee's whistle now. She clenched her fists, then stiffened her arms against the seat of her chair. She pushed herself up an inch or two. Her face flushed, jaw set, eyes narrowed. "We do not talk about such things."

Virginia and I sat in stunned silence. Mom rose, pushed her chair back, and departed for the den. A moment later, the TV blared. "It's a long putt for a birdie on the twelfth. Let's see if he can make it."

There was no more talk of Dad. Not then. Not ever.

Chapter 24

Wendy invades my daydreams and my night dreams. She smiles at me the moment I awaken. The piece of paper with her name and phone number sits on my desk. I stare at the print as if the letters were her. As if they had magic in them. And they do. When did my heart last smile like this? Her arms leap off the page and reach up to me. They are there, even when they are not there. She sits across from me at breakfast, then rides in my passenger seat as I head to work, never more than a blink away.

My hand shakes as I reach for the phone. She answers on the third ring. We set up a date to go dancing, Friday after next.

The sun rises and the sun sets and the clock ticks and the days dribble by. On the Tuesday before the Friday, I come down with a cold. It will pass. It has to. It doesn't. I call Wendy, "I'm feeling better but I don't have the energy for a night of dancing. If you're up for it, we could go out to dinner?"

"I'm sorry..."

My heart sinks. *Okay, she doesn't want to go to dinner. I can't blame her.* The next words that flow from the telephone are a soft salve that she rubs all over me.

"...that you don't feel well. If you're sure you're up to it, dinner would be fun."

We meet at The Frog and the Peach at seven o'clock. It's one of those perfect, early spring evenings when the sun seems to linger in the sky past its expected bedtime, just to light our way. The leaves on the eucalyptus trees shimmer in electric anticipation and the street is filled with the smells of peanut sauce and a hundred other Indian spices. Who could not stop to bow at the wonder of life.

I'm twenty minutes early. Wendy arrives right on time, like a field of Van Gogh's sunflowers bursting into bloom before my eyes. The fullness of life I'd felt when I watched her at the disco party burns inside me. We sit next to each other in a quiet, cozy booth, in the corner, perfect. I read the menu over three times, top to bottom, bottom to top, random starts and stops. I could read it ten times in ten ways and still not understand a word. I slip over toward her, an inch or two. How close do I dare? We order grilled something garnished with an anything sauce and two glasses of whatever, then we toast. "To us" I want to say, but it's premature. "To dancing," I suggest.

"To dancing." She smiles. This is not about toasts and words.

The doubt I am so used to carrying around with me disappears. In its place, an uncharacteristic boldness. "Your dancing was electric."

She gazes at me, like she's not quite sure what to do with my comment. "Well, thank you. Do you go out dancing often?"

"Not so often."

"But you wanted to go out dancing again?" It is half statement, half musing.

"I wanted to go out dancing *with you*," I say. I have crossed a threshold. No turning back now.

She nods pensively, letting my words sink in. We move on, talk a little about our experiences on the hotline, then begin to share our life stories. She leans forward, eyes locked on mine, smiling from time to time, listening not just to my words, but to my soul. She asks a thousand questions. Why and when and how frequently, and how did you feel about that? That's what she wants most to know. How did I feel? She probes and prods, digging to understand, so different from most people who are mostly waiting for a way to turn the conversation back to themselves. I talk on, then try to get her to tell her story, but she has more and still more questions for me. Finally, she tells me the basics: she's a teacher for the visually impaired, working with the San Francisco Unified School District. She describes her family and upbringing in Southern California, one younger, married sister and a brother who died in childhood, parents still living in Pasadena. "And where do you live in Marin?" I ask.

"We're in Mill Valley."

"We." The word pierces my chest, a cutting blast of arctic air. "We." Two letters. Two stabs. Of course, the man at the party, the one in the car. I had banished him so quickly from my mind. I feel myself pull back, an inch or two on the bench, a mile or two in my mind. "Who is we?"

"My husband, Greg. Two sons. Doug is six, Gavin four."

Is this how it feels when the doctor announces that you have an incurable disease? Why didn't I think? Why didn't

I realize? How blind am I? How foolish. I showed up at the right party, but a decade late.

"Tell me more about them. Your family?"

She shows me pictures of the boys. "And Greg?"

She pushes her food around the plate, then puts her fork down. I watch her eyes for some hint. They soften, hold my gaze, but I can't read the message. "It's hard to talk about."

"It's hard to hear about." I look out, beyond our table, aware for the first time that there is a room out there, other people, lots of them. A party of eight at a table near us, young couples, drinking and laughing. I don't feel like laughing.

Wendy frowns. "What's that supposed to mean?"

"I feel foolish. You wear a ring. I should have known, or at least wondered, but I was so captivated, I never thought about it. If you don't want to talk about it…It's none of my business."

"We have a good marriage," she says. She puckers her lips, unbuttons the top button on her yellow sweater, then pulls her sweater tighter around her. She's silent. I wait. "We had a…" Wendy's turn to look out at the other people in the restaurant. I am suspended over a precipice. "The past couple of years have been very hard. We're in counseling now."

"Trying to put it back together?"

She looks down, pushes some food around her plate. "I guess that's what we're doing. I was motivated at the beginning. When we got married, I'd never have believed we'd be in the mess we're in now. Our therapist says we're locked in a massive power struggle. Maybe she's given up on us too."

"Given up?" Who's given up? Given up on marriage? On love? On Greg? But you're still married? Do you love him? Could you ever love me? So many questions. I grab for one. "How long have you been married?" I ask. Not the question I want to ask at all.

"Relationships are so hard," she says.

I scan my own desert history, a cactus growing here and there. The sharp thorns are most prominent.

"For the first few years, we saved our money so we could travel," she continues. "We were young and free, and we wanted to see the world. Africa, India, Europe. We visited the Masai in Kenya, travelled down the Nile on a barge loaded with camels, and bicycled the coast of Yugoslavia. It was amazing, then when we came home, we were ready to start a family. The boys were born. We bought a house. It was perfect until it suddenly wasn't. It's hard even to say what happened." Her lips open and close. "I was the center of his world, and then, I don't know, it all changed."

Words tumble out, important words, but even as she pauses to see how I'll react, even as she closes her mouth and frowns slightly, waiting for my reply, then brushes her hair back in awkward shyness, even then I have no response because I have no idea what she is saying. My world has shrunk, time and space collapsing until there is nothing beyond my desire to hold her in my arms and kiss those soft, sweet lips. Her hand rests on the table, small and perfect. It's all I can do not to take it in mine and lift it to my mouth, to kiss each finger and turn it over and run my fingers up hers and down into the crevice and to the next and up and down, soft and slow and sensuous like the whisper of blossoms in spring. Our hands are just inches apart. It would be such a simple gesture, but this hand is not mine to hold. Our hands are still miles apart. We lapse into a soft sound, like rain on the roof at night, when you wake up from a dream and you're not quite sure what is real and what is fantasy.

A waiter dressed in black stands so close to our table he is almost sitting on it. "Excuse me, but we're cleaning up, ready to close." He slides the check under a plate. I look around the restaurant. Chairs are stacked on the tables. Someone is mopping the floor. The table of eight, all the other customers, have vanished into the night. We look at our plates, look at each other, and break into synchronous laughter. Neither of us has even tasted our whatever food.

"Would you like a box to go?" the waiter asks.

"No. I'm sure it's good," Wendy says. "We had a lot to talk about."

Outside, the streets are quiet. A couple ambles along arm in arm. I start to put my arm in Wendy's, but pull back. "Can I walk you to your car?"

She nods. When we get to her car, I reach over and take her hand. I know the right thing to say. I hear every word in my mind. *I wish you well with your marriage counseling. If things ever don't work out, I mean if you decide to split up, and if you'd be interested, you have my number on the hotline roster. I'd love to hear from you. I mean I'd love to see you. I mean I love you, and . . . No, that last part will never do. But up to there, yes, that's it.* After giving my speech, I'd walk away and not look back, sad but knowing I'd done the right thing. I'd walk as fast as I could to my car and I'd drive home and go back to work the next day and the next and the next and work and work and forget that we ever met and that this evening ever happened and put her out of my mind. I have the speech all ready, but when I open my mouth, the words I have rehearsed scatter, across the sea, lost forever. "This has been such a wonderful evening, better than I could possibly have imagined. Can I see you again?"

I have heard newly pregnant women talk about walking around, glowing, filled to the brim by the secret that no one else knows. If that's how it is, then I'm as close to being pregnant as I'll ever be. Our secret dwells inside me, like a warm fire on a cold night. I feel it in my belly. Every thought I have, I want to share with her. I fantasize my arms about her. I can feel the warmth of her body, the smoothness of her skin, the curve of her neck, the easy way we fit together.

It is the moment of separation. Wendy's smile starts at the corners of her mouth and spreads across her face, like the sun peeking over the horizon in the morning. "Yes. I'll call."

"When?" I ask.

"Soon."

✱

She comes over to my house the following week. Standing just inside the front door, the first words out of her mouth, "I told Greg."

Moments later, she is sitting on my bed. I stand by the window. "What did you tell him?"

"I told him about our dinner. I told him I wanted to keep seeing you."

"And what did he say?"

"He asked me not to."

"And you said?"

"That I was going to keep seeing you." She looks down at the floor. "We've been sleeping in separate bedrooms since."

How rapidly the rules change. I am overjoyed. I am petrified. I am guilty as charged. I have fallen down the rabbit hole and found myself, like Alice, in a new world. A moment's passion has thrust me into a drama with serious overtones. I am used to a no-strings dating game that could be called off easily by either party. I've never been involved with a married woman. I respect the sanctity of marriage and respect myself for respecting it. Suddenly I am with a woman who is not just married but married with children. Two of them. Very young ones. My euphoria wobbles. My doubts surge.

And yet, when I put my arms around Wendy and we lie down next to each other, we fit together so seamlessly, as if our relationship had been polished over the years. It shines with a freshness that is intense, raw, and exciting. I shove the delicacies of the situation into the nether regions of my mind and swim joyously with this woman who instinctively knows how to light my fire. How could something this good be anything but right?

There is a primordial quality about our attraction that is irresistible. Call it fate or karma or destiny. Call it the alignment of the stars, the wheel of fortune, the collective unconscious, the force, the writing on the wall, or even God's will. Call it all of these. Call it none of these. Call it the wisdom of the heart, or maybe its stubbornness. Or its foolishness. Maybe it is Eros up to his old tricks. Cupid and his bow. So many words. Words don't matter.

But the words do matter, because they hint at the deeper

questions of life. Who is in control? Is anyone in control? Is this mere coincidence? Are we nothing more than flotsam and jetsam randomly tossed about by the storms of the universe? Am I still a rat, madly pressing the bar in one of Professor Temple's cages? Drip, drip goes the testosterone. Are we clanging hormones, machines responding to the on/off switch programmed millions of years ago? Are we puppets responding to strings manipulated by some greater god? Metaphorically, I am totally with such myth, but I am a staunch skeptic when it comes to any literal acceptance of these so-called forces of the universe. I recognize the biological urge, but I cling also—desperately?—to the idea of choice, and therefore responsibility. We are raging hormones, and we are more than raging hormones.

Or are we?

In mythology, Eros is pictured often as a cherubic child or an impossibly handsome stud, the winged male. Neither of these are my Eros. My Eros is more like a fat Buddha, hands clasped over his belly, doubled over in laughter, tears streaming down his cheeks as he points at me and exclaims, "Man, you are one fucked-up dude who needs some serious help. I know just the woman who can do it, and I'm sending her your way."

✱

When the phone rings, I know it is her. Some things you just know. Besides, it's after nine o'clock at night. I figure she's had time to put the kids to bed, and Greg is busy with something, so she can get off by herself. I almost answer the phone "Hi, Wendy," but since I live in a group house and we get lots of phone calls, I err on the side of caution.

"Hello."

"Hello, is this Peter?" A man's voice. Not Wendy.

"Yes. Who is this?"

"This is Greg, Wendy's husband."

I am stunned into silence. I wait.

"Wendy told me. I'd like to talk."

Chapter 25

Greg and I meet on a blustery day, in the late afternoon, outside the entrance to the Red Hill Shopping Center in San Anselmo. We've never spoken, never met before. I size him up. He sizes me up. His hair is shorter than mine, but otherwise we might be old college buddies stopping for a chat. Or he could be the brother I never had. We shake hands, then sit on a low brick wall just above the street.

Wind groans in angry outbursts through the elms along Sir Francis Drake Boulevard. Clouds scuttle by overhead. A man cradling a bouquet of lilies scurries by.

Greg wastes no time on small talk. "I'd like you to stop seeing Wendy."

His words take my breath away. I'm like a man who's walked outside, expecting a normal day, only to find a truck bearing down, about to crush him. What did I expect, an invitation to dinner? In the few short weeks that Wendy and I have had together, she has pricked my bubble of loneliness as no one else ever has. In her presence, the sadness falls away. I am no longer a leaf blowing in the wind. I am part of a tree. I might even be part of a family. I have fantasized about a life together with her. I've watched us walking down the street together. Watched us talking, playing, planning, loving. The idea of having a soul mate is one I'd never permitted myself before. Amazing how quickly the psyche can enroll in a new vision. If it fits. And this one fits.

How will I answer? The moment calls for wisdom, truth, and gravitas. I am filled with doubt and fear. She is his wife. There are children, two. She is my—my what? My hope. How far can you go on hope? She gives a lot, but she wants a lot in return, perhaps more than I know how to give. I've lived my whole life in a cave. It's how my mother lives. It's how my father lived. It's lonely, but it's known. So many issues. I haven't even met her children. It's a package deal, I realize that. I have been single for so long. The thought of this kind of responsibility scares me. I have a good job, but I don't have a lot of savings. I don't own a home. And what about sexual freedom? If the past is any predictor of the future, I am a serial monogamist. This relationship is on a different level. Am I ready? Or am I too late? There is the fear and there is the doubt and there is the hope. And there is the guilt. I've always said I believed in marriage. Am I breaking up a family? Or am I helping to pick up the pieces?

Greg and I sit on opposite sides of the brick wall, like two cats squaring off. He stares at me. He wants an answer.

"It's difficult."

He doesn't respond. I try to read his mind. I peer inside myself. What's the likelihood of things ever working out between Wendy and me? We have a strong connection, but we're programmed for that kind of thing. The chances of a lasting relationship? Who knows? And is that even what I want?

Greg squints, turns toward me. His voice is laced with impatience. "I can't make you stop seeing her. I'm asking."

I search the clouds overhead, as if the answer were embedded above. My mind balks. My heart races. I have to say something. What should I say?

"Yes," I say.

"Yes?" he repeats. "What do you mean?"

My head and my heart face off, boxers in the ring, on my left, in the dark trunks, weighing 180 pounds, Doubt, and on my right, in the light trunks, Love. Doubt enters the ring, opens with a one-two punch, trying to win the fight before it gets started. It's all wrong. She's married. She has children, two of them. You're not ready, you've said it yourself. You prize your freedom. Get out of here while you can. I nod. Yes, yes, but then Love sneaks around to the back door. Wendy dances in front of me. I taste the times we've already had, imagine what it might be like. The cold, lonely nights and how sweet it could be. I trace the shape of her lips, run my finger down the bridge of her nose. Feel her arms around me. All this happens in a tenth of a second. But wait. Someone else enters the ring. It's a woman. An older woman. Gray hair, a perm, a worried look. Dressed in a pleated, calf-length skirt. One eye is drooped. It's Mom.

"Mom, what are you doing here?"

"She's a married woman. Be strong. Walk away."

"Yes, I'll stop seeing her." The words are out of my mouth before I understand what I'm saying. I reach out, trying to capture them in midair. No, come back. I don't mean it. Too late.

Greg looks at me with a mixture of suspicion and delight. "You'll stop seeing her?"

"That's what I said."

"Thank you." He offers his hand. I shake it.

I nod, start, on automatic, to say, "You're welcome," but stop myself. Welcome for what? Your wife.

He looks me in the eye. I rush in to fill the silence. "Looks like it might rain." Such an inane comment. Here we are, playing chess for life. He turns to leave.

"One more thing," I say.

He nods.

"I want to be the one to tell her."

His nod is slower this time.

"I'll call her today." I check my watch. The whole conversation has taken less than ten minutes.

When I get home, I call Wendy as agreed. This has to be done. She cries. I shut down my heart, the way I was taught. Easier that way. Better. Perhaps. Rats, conditioned rats.

Chapter 26

Indecision is doubt's stillborn child.

Without Wendy in my life, nothing sparkles—not my bedroom, not my car, not the trail where we hiked, certainly not my hopes and my dreams. I bury my head in my pillow, soak up her sweet scent. She left a sock behind. I keep it under my pillow, fondle it, turn it over, as if it could bring her back. As if it were a gift. Not the gift, it's the giver that matters. The closeness we might have had someday, the home, the stories to share, the family, all I want, the light, the warmth, the love we could have brought each other—gone. I drive by her neighborhood hoping to catch a glimpse, but wary. What if he spots me instead?

At work, I can't concentrate. "Time," friends counsel me. "Time heals." They are wrong. Time makes a good wine better. She was the best already. Why did I give in so fast? I try to picture what they are doing. Are they back in counseling again? Do they make love? Or have they realized it's over, and have I lost out needlessly? I am such a dunce. I hate that phrase. It is Mom's voice, not mine. And who made that decision anyway? Was it Mom? I love my mother, but I hate it when I think like her. I am not a dunce. I am a mixed-up, confused guy who made a rotten

222   *Peter Gibb*

decision. The situation called for boldness. I called up my wimpiness. Or was I trying honestly to do the right thing? Or is that an excuse, masking the reality that I was afraid? I threw away my one chance for happiness. Maybe I am a dunce after all.

I pick up the phone and dial the first few digits, then hang up. I can't go back. I made a decision, gave my word.

Then one morning, the telephone grabs my hand and all but dials itself. After four rings, an answering machine clicks on. "We are not at home. Please leave a message for Wendy or Greg. We'll call you back." Too much "we." "*We* are not at home. *We* will call you back." Of course, I don't leave a message, but I have crossed the river, and there is no going back. Calling again later is easy. She answers on the second ring.

"Hi, Wendy. This is Peter."

A moment of silence. She can't have forgotten. Perhaps she is angry that I'm calling after I promised not to? Or maybe he is there, standing next to her. Maybe they were in bed. Is there a phone by the bed?

"Peter!" The sun shines through her voice. I've never been so happy to hear my own name spoken.

"I've missed you so much." The words tumble out of my mouth. I flush. Is it too much? Will I scare her?

"Yes, me too." The warmth in her voice curls around me.

"I don't know how to say this." *Then say it. Out with it.* "I made a terrible mistake. I don't know what's happening with you now, but if you...if you're interested, I'd like to...I want to see you again."

There I've said it.

The next two words are the sweetest I've ever heard. "Oh, yes."

We begin an experiment. No guarantees, no assurances. Just hope, and a landscape of desire. We meet once furtively, but Wendy is not one for cheating, secrets, or subterfuge. "I have to tell Greg."

"What will he say?"

"He'll be mad."

"That's not good," I say.

Wendy pauses, but briefly. "It'll be hard. I'll deal with it."

It's a new language for me. Instead of hiding from problems, you talk about them, deal with them. Direct, clear, scary. The way I'd like to be, not the way I am, certainly not the way I was brought up.

Wendy and I start to see each other, infrequently but regularly. It's not all easy. I have lived so long in solitary. I know a little about romance, very little about love, and nothing about intimacy. I want it. I don't want it. I love it. I am scared of it. I am like the little shorebirds that patter into the waves, then upon discovering how wet the water is, retreat quickly.

Wendy joins me at our San Anselmo communal home for an early-afternoon liaison, our time, as always, rushed. We lie in bed together. "How was that for you?" she asks.

"Good." I turn away. I need time. I need space. I don't know why. It was good, but now I want to crawl back into my cave. Hiding in the cave is my natural condition.

Wendy wants pillow talk. "I feel so close to you. Can we cuddle a bit?"

I glance at the clock. "It's after two. I promised to call

Cindy at work to confirm our travel plans for tomorrow. I totally forgot."

"Cindy? Again."

"It'll take two minutes."

"I just want to hold you."

I jump out of bed. What I thought would be a two-minute call morphs into a twenty-minute strategy session. When I return, the bed is empty.

We repair the damage in ten-minute stolen phone calls. Over the next several months, we continue to meet, all too briefly, for hurried kisses and conversations that want to linger and flow but instead are forced to jump and run. One Saturday she's able to arrange a whole afternoon just for the two of us. I invite her for a hike. We start at the Pantoll Ranger Station and hike along the Matt Davis Trail on Mt. Tamalpais. It's a magnificent day. I've packed the picnic to end all picnics: engraved wineglasses and a bottle of chardonnay from Clos Du Val Winery in Napa, a German buttermilk blue cheese and some creamy brie, an artichoke and roasted garlic dip, a caramelized red onion and fig dip, sourdough baguettes, crackers, cloth napkins, and my special blanket that I carried on my back, hitchhiking home from Peru. I am no gourmet chef, but this is one worthy picnic. I have planned and fantasized the time we will have, eating and drinking beyond any reasonable limit and then rolling up inside my blanket for the longest kiss in history. I have chosen the spot. We head out the trail. It's a gorgeous day. You can see forever. The ocean is calm, the sky is blue, and I'm in love.

Once we get to the coast, I put down the picnic basket and unroll the blanket. "Here we are."

Wendy frowns. "We can't stop here. We haven't had a hike yet."

"Look what I brought." I'm on my knees spreading the blanket. I pull out the chardonnay.

"Aren't you forgetting something?" For a minute, I think I hear my mother, then it's Wendy again, "You said we were going to hike, and then picnic."

"We hiked. It's time for the wine and cheese."

Wendy frowns. "You call that a hike?"

I cock my head, simulating serious internal debate. "Yes, I do."

"Doug hikes farther than that. He's six."

"I know how old Doug is."

"You don't know how far he hikes."

I pour myself a glass of wine, spread a piece of the baguette with the German blue cheese, lie back on the blanket. "Want some?" The cheese is tasty. Wendy is quiet, but the wheels are turning. "So you're having your picnic now?"

"I am."

"No hike?"

"We had a hike."

"That wasn't a hike."

"Okay, call it whatever, how about hikenic?"

Wendy tosses me a lame smile. "The blanket's big enough for two," I invite her, sweeping my hand across the picnic spread. I turn my palms up, shrug my shoulders, in false magnanimity. "Who arranged this outing? Who brought the picnic?" Silence descends. "Sit down and have some wine." My voice is half invitation, half command. My rusty heart senses an advantage and tries to drive it home. "Flexibility is a virtue."

She doesn't respond. "I want to hike a bit farther. I'll be back in a while."

"A while? Ten minutes? An hour?"

"I don't know." A turkey buzzard circles overhead.

Wendy steps back, then turns, and starts walking. I watch her grow smaller, around a bend, then gone. Anger growls inside me. I finish the glass of wine and pour another, spread some cheese. *She doesn't care about my picnic. So what, I'll eat it. I'm hungry. I have things to do at home. I planned the picnic. It was my picnic. I didn't want to stay out here all afternoon anyway.* The wine is open, half gone. I pour another glass and gulp it down. I put the bottle down on the blanket. I want more. I grab the glass. My foot hits the bottle. Over it goes. "Shit." I grab the bottle but knock over the glass. A squirrel darts by, stops, inspects, turns, scampers away. Blue sky still above. What a joke. The picnic. Why did I bother? I lie back. Close my eyes. Maybe this was all a mistake? Maybe I don't belong. My heart grinds.

"I'm back." She drops her backpack on the blanket, like she's moving in. "It was so beautiful up there. I could see all the way to the Farallon Islands."

I glance her way. "It was beautiful here too." Without you, I want to say it, but I hold my tongue. She sits down. "Any cheese left?"

I point at the cheese. She waits for me to slice it. I don't. She does. She begins her play-by-play. "Lots of wildflowers—lupine and poppies and a lovely orange-red one I've never seen before." She goes on, but I don't hear what she's saying. I don't even try. The wall goes up. She stops her report. "Why are you so upset?"

"Why are you so self-righteous?" The words tumble out as if by their own momentum. I planned a peaceful picnic in a beautiful place and this is what I get for my troubles. She holds out a glass.

"It's gone," I say.

"Empty! You drank the whole bottle?"

"It spilled."

"How'd that happen?"

"Spilled. You know, angles, geometry. It tipped over."

Silence rides with us, a third passenger in the front seat as we drive home. We pull into the parking lot where she left her car. She collects her broken dreams and exits in silence. "See you 'round the county."

The car door clicks shut. She is gone.

Once home, I am all business—calendars and work plans and plane tickets. The next day, I fly to Minneapolis for my first Interaction Associates solo consulting job, nervous but excited. Alone in the hotel, I review my agenda for the next day, then slip into the hotel bed.

Wendy immediately rushes in. My thoughts crawl back to the picnic. What happened? I remember being upset, her walking away, but the story I tell myself makes no sense. I want to call her. Of course, I can't. I want to wrap my arms around her. Of course, I can't. The tape of her vanishing along the trail plays in my mind. She turns at the last minute, one last glance, a glance I interpret as disgust—or is it confusion? or maybe just hurt?—and then she disappears around the corner, gone, only to reappear and walk away again, and gone, and away, over and over as if to drive home some point that I am too confused to absorb. What did I say when we parted? "See you 'round the county," as if it were some casual "See you later" or some definitive "Maybe I'll never see you again." Are we still friends? Are we still lovers? What did she think I meant? What did I mean? What were we really fighting about? How is it possible? I can't even remember what we were fighting about. The anger has dissipated. But regret and shame stick to me like the lingering smell of a long dead animal. I am so far from the open, loving, peace-filled being I aspire to be.

On the flight home from Minneapolis, I think about nothing but Wendy. I write about her in my journal. I imagine calling her. I have never felt this way about a woman. It is so clear to me. I want to be with her. Why did we fight? Missing her, the ache deep in my stomach, like the death rattle from a dying animal. How could I be so stupid? I consider driving straight to her house and proposing that she move out of her house, bring the kids, and move in with me. Why did we squabble? What would happen if I went to her house and knocked on her door? No, not at ten o'clock at night, to a married woman, a mother who's not expecting me. But the instant I'm home, I sit at my desk and write her a letter. I apologize for my behavior on the mountain. I tell her as honestly as I can how much I miss her, how lonely I am for her, how unsettled my life is, but that if she will have me—even though it's complicated—I want to keep seeing her. In the morning I rush to the post office to be sure my letter is on its way first thing. The post office promises she will receive it the next day. Once I've mailed it, I feel better. It's awkward. I live on hope.

We patch and repair like an old married couple. I want

to be with her, but I have lived my whole life alone. I have so much to learn. Greg moves out. Six months later, I move in. I have an instant family—just stir in love. Doug accepts the new arrangement with little or no resistance. Gavin is more cautious. It takes time, everyone says. I hope they're right.

Wendy's divorce finalizes. Neither of us wants to jump right into marriage, but the issue hovers outside the bedroom window. One day, Wendy has a wry smile on her face, "I'll tell you when I'm ready for you to propose." We both laugh. I'm feeling the same: not quite ready, but soon.

Four months later she says, "I'm ready."

Three weeks later, I say, "Will you...?"

Two seconds later, she says, "Yes."

We celebrate with a simple ceremony, her family and mine, in our home. A month or so before the wedding, Doug says to me, "As soon as you're married, I'm going to start calling you 'Dad.'" My eyes tear up. I am thirty-nine years old. Two years ago I was a lonely, lost boy on a career track to nowhere. Now I'm married to the most wonderful woman possible, cofather of two great boys, established in a career I believe in, working and living with people I love. Glory hallelujah!

But a photo from the wedding tells a more troubled story: Wendy on one side, me on the other, with Gavin in the middle, arms outstretched, pushing us apart with all his six year-old might, his world shattered.

I am the shatterer.

In the spirit of family, we take Doug and Gavin on our honeymoon to Hawaii. Dumb. Honeymoon is about romance and coupledom. Young children are not interested in romance and coupledom. Doug and Gavin want to play all day in the elevator. We have different games in mind. It is not a good mix.

I am surrounded by the outward manifestations of everything I want, but peace is never that easy. Doubts about myself undermine my every move. It's still the old world of doubt: how long before they realize that I'm a fraud?

✶

We've been married five months. We're standing in the kitchen, washing up after dinner. The boys are downstairs playing fort. I've been putting this off for a few days, searching for the right time. "I'm leaving Monday for a job in Nevada, three days." I toss the news out casually.

"Oh." An arctic blast blows across the kitchen counter. "What's the job?" she asks, closing the dishwasher with a little more force than necessary.

"I've mentioned it to you before. The federal project, choosing a site for nuclear waste disposal." I turn the water back on, re-rinse a glass I've already washed and dried. "The issues are so complex, so many competing points of view. Nobody wants nuclear waste in their backyard, but if we're going to have nuclear energy, the waste has to go somewhere. At the last meeting someone suggested we blast it into space. You know, they're seriously considering it. We've sufficiently polluted the world. Now let's take on space. What will they think?"

Wendy folds the dish towel neatly into thirds. "The job with Cindy?" she interrupts my rambling.

"It was a novel idea, at least. Poison the aliens. Why not?" My joke falls flat on the counter.

She lays the dish towel down, manipulating it until it is parallel to the sink, exactly one inch from the edge. "You just went on a job with her."

"That was two weeks ago."

"Why do you always work with Cindy?"

"Why are you so suspicious?"

"You travel with her. You're with her all day. What do you do at night? You have dinner together, I suppose." She picks up the dish towel, turns it over and folds it, again.

"Usually, sure." I go hot all over. "I have a job to do. That's all. I like Cindy. I respect her."

"Do you have wine?"

"What difference does it make whether we have wine or not?"

"We? You order together?"

"We. Me. I don't know who orders what."

"So you do?"

"Do what?"

"Order together."

"Look, there's nothing going on between Cindy and me." I feel my face tightening, my ribs rattling. "Absolutely nothing! Can you hear that?"

"Shh. I don't want the boys to hear."

"Don't *shh* me. You're the one who brought up this whole absurd fantasy in the first place."

"I need to know."

"I work with Cindy. That's all there is to know. We're friends and colleagues. Nothing more." I feel the walls closing in around me. What I most feared. I will not let a woman control me. Tears begin to dribble down her cheeks. She's like Mom. The same quivering lips and voice.

Just like Mom when she wants something totally irrational, the tears, the ultimate weapon for manipulation. My heart closes, the thud of the steel door. "Pull yourself together, would you."

"Thanks, Peter. Thanks for your understanding and support."

"You're so welcome." We play matching sarcasm.

Then she gets quiet. Her eyes drop. The game is over. A moment later, the bedroom door shuts, a little click. Why doesn't she at least slam it? Muffled sobs leak out under the door. I know what she wants. She wants me to crawl in there on my knees. *Well, I am not going to do that. She can cry all night long if that's what she wants.* I have to pack tonight and be ready to leave in the morning. I finish the dishes. Somebody has to hold it together in this family. I check downstairs to see if Doug and Gavin are okay. They're happily still playing fort in the bedroom, oblivious of the real war raging upstairs. Good. I pull the big gray suitcase from the closet. Shit, it ripped on the last trip. I have to find the duct tape to mend it. *She is so infuriating! Jealousy is such a waste of energy.* Just like Mom's fits, when Dad smiled and was friendly with Mazie. Innocent as could be. My mind swirls around, going nowhere, spinning faster and faster: Wendy, Cindy, Mom, jealousy, work, control, married, single, tears, fears, doubt, doubt, doubt. *I'll sleep in the guest room, get up and out of here in the morning, not even have to see her.*

"I'm sorry." She's standing in the doorway, in her night-gown, the hallway light behind her. I can see right through her nightgown. She looks so small.

"Sorry?"

"It's just...when you go away, and I know you're together and working on things you care about, and she's so bright and pretty and interesting and I know what can happen, and—"

"What can happen? What do you think is happening?"

"If you want to end it now, I'd understand."

"What's that supposed to mean?"

"Just what I said. We can end it now. I'm no good at relationships."

I throw the socks I'm packing on the floor. "Jesus."

She cringes. Wendy isn't religious, but she is protective of Jesus.

"Jesus," I repeat, under my breath this time. Disgust wells up inside me, fills my cavities, and spills out my pores. She looks down. My eyes follow. Her feet are bare. It's cold. She folds her arms across her chest, shivers. I pull a sweater from the suitcase and toss it to her. She slips it over her head. "Thanks."

When she bends over to pick up a piece of lint off the floor, my eyes follow the line and the dance as the hem of her nightdress rides slowly, seductively, up her calf, and suddenly, I am on the Ferris wheel, a child again, a man-child this time, spinning faster and higher as I did once years before, floating in a cauldron of desire, drinking in her face that glistens with sparkling tears, and her tender eyes, and a mouth made from passion, a woman that I must, this instant, hold and caress until I am no more, lost in the forever, a man in lust and love. I grasp the smooth curve of her back and feel the instant swelling inside me. She rises to her tiptoes and scoops her arms around my neck. She nestles her head on my shoulder. I press my body tight against hers. I merge softly into the web of oneness, where I am so much more than me, something that kisses the nature of existence and drinks it in, beyond mind and beyond body, devil it may be, or angel, or god, beyond word, beyond sound, beyond light, lost and found and happy.

Chapter 27

The four of us—Wendy, Doug, Gavin and I—become a family. We play games, get a dog, plant trees, build a tree house. We eat together, hike together, have weekly family meetings together (resisted by the kids, promoted by the parents). Wendy is all heart. I'm all head. The boys are all kid. Doug and Gavin spend one week with us, then a week with Greg. For the most part, the arrangement works well. Wendy and I have a week to be a couple alone, then a week with kids. I see Greg when he comes to pick up the boys, and soon grow to like and appreciate him. I am learning, making friends, and making a decent living doing work I believe in. I'm the happiest I've ever been, but something is still missing. Something inside knocks at me. I want to connect at a deeper level, but before I can do that, I have to connect with myself. Familiar, unnaturally dark moods still show up uninvited at my front door.

Despite many hours of therapy and personal-growth workshops, I am a jumble of doubt in search of a person. Mom whispers in my ear, scolding me, advising me, drowning out my voice with hers. "I am such a dunce," she says. I say it too. I think the way my mother thinks, talk the way she talks. She's in my closet when I get dressed in the morning and there when I hang up my clothes at night. I walk like her and talk like her. Maybe Professor Temple was right: I am a conditioned rat.

I love and appreciate my parents. They've given me a home where I am safe and secure. I've never wanted for material comfort. Even though no one ever says so, I know I was loved. My parents are not alcoholics or drug addicts, gangsters or abusers. I love and resent my parents, in the same breath. Most of all, I want Mom to be my mother, not my alter ego.

I hear about an intensive growth experience, the Fisher-Hoffman Quadrinity Process, that seems designed for people with overly intrusive parental voices in their heads. When I check to see what others say about it, I hear words such as "brutal," "shocking," "extreme," "radical." And the only word I care about: "effective." The twelve-week class is outrageously expensive, but I desperately want to dispense with this mother shadow that eats me away from inside. If it works, it's worth it. Wendy and I sign up together. We both have "parent issues." Who doesn't?

Eighteen of us gather in a drab meeting room for our first intensive weekend. I can hear the nerves rattling. Under other circumstances I can imagine being friends with my very British instructor, Dorothea, but she is all business. She demands five thousand words a week, every intimate detail about how my parents "abused" me.

"I love my parents," I tell her.

"How long have you been stuck in your life?" she deadpans. "How long have you been following your parents' direction, playing out their tapes, cowering from your own potential, afraid to go beyond their limited horizons?"

I shake my head. "They did the best they could. They—"

"The choice is yours," Dorothea cuts me off. "Stay stuck if that's how you want to live your life. But stop wasting my time. And yours."

Quadrinity is like using a chainsaw to split toothpicks. It's brutal, but I've paid all this money. I recognize that this may be my last, best chance to erase my fraud story and claim my own soul. I bring in an overstuffed pillow that is to represent each of my parents in turn. I beat the pillow with a bat and yell and scream at it. I work myself into a frenzy. "I hate you. Mom. You fucked up my life. I hate you. I hate you. I don't even know who I am."

"Smack her," Dorothea demands from behind me. "Whack her again. Harder."

I puff and sweat as I drink a wild cocktail of guilt and liberation.

"Harder," Dorothea demands. "I can't see the anger."

How can I do this to my parents who loved and cared for me? If they knew what I was doing . . . They were never cruel to me. Dorothea gets my ambivalence. "We have an expression for people like you, pussy-footers." She goes on to explain. "We are all guilty, but no one is to blame." Slowly I come to understand. My parents messed up. All parents mess up. It's the nature of power, the dance of the generations. All children either rebel or imitate their parents. Both paths are reactionary; neither works. You have to metaphorically kill your parents. So you can be free to love them.

It's a bizarre approach, but by the end of the twelve weeks, I feel strangely reborn. I may not know who I am, but I am not my mother. I can finally appreciate and love my mother and father for who they are, forgive them for who they are not, and get on with my life. It is a decisive victory in a forty-year-long war.

✱

At dinner, Wendy pours me a glass of wine. "Thanks, aren't you having some?" I ask.

She pours herself a glass of water. That smile—something different. I've never seen it before. She sets five tall green candles on the table. We often eat by candlelight, usually two or three votives.

"Why the special candles?" I ask.

"Guess."

"I've no idea."

"Five candles," she tilts her head in suggestive disappointment. "One for you and one for me and one for Doug and one for Gavin."

"That's four," I say. Then it hits me. My eyes pop. I look at her, entreating, but not daring to speak. She nods. "I think it was when we were at Lake Tahoe," she says. I remember the time, how passionate I'd felt, but I never dared imagine. Once married, we'd relaxed about birth control. We'd talked about having a baby but never made the decision. Our joyous yell rocks the neighborhood for weeks.

A month later, Wendy calls me at work. "It's a girl." Love, like a river, fills me. Tears pour down my cheeks. I rush home to celebrate. That evening we begin work on the nursery.

The pregnancy consumes us. Everything goes so right, until it goes wrong. At twenty-eight weeks, with the nursery half finished and baby clothes piling up, Wendy wakes up one night with contractions. The frequency is increasing. A call to the hospital is met with a no-nonsense reply, "Bring her in right away." Dr. Granton, a stern-faced OB/GYN, examines her.

"It looks like premature labor," she says. "Can't be sure, but at this stage, it's touch and go. The lungs are very under-developed. The fetus might be viable."

"Viable?" I know the word, but in this context?

"It might survive."

"She," I correct.

"We'll start Wendy on terbutaline," Dr. Granton continues, "to try to reduce the contractions, and other medication to hasten the development of the baby's lungs. We'll do all we can. No promises."

"Viable." I repeat the word as if it has some special power. The doc peers at us through her tortoiseshell glasses, concealing any recognizable emotion. "Every day we can hold off improves the odds. You should tour the preemie ward, so you see what you might be getting in for."

The preemie ward is eerily silent. With Wendy confined to bed, I join parents, humbled in hope and prayer, watching over tiny incubators. The diminutive beings inside teeter on the edge of life, bandaged and tubed, eyes closed, so still it's hard to be sure they are even alive, so new in their skin, so fragile. Most of the babies would fit in the palm of one hand, eight tiny beings, their eyelids thin as butterfly wings, flickering a message, "Please, give me a chance."

We return home, but the contractions start again. Back in the hospital, Wendy rolls over, mumbles something incomprehensible, then turns bone white. A nurse rushes to her aid. She presses a button and the room fills with white coats. An oxygen mask appears from nowhere. Anxious eyes search the monitor.

Ten minutes later it's over. "She was on her way out," the doctor says. "Blood pressure sixty over zero. I think it's the terbutaline."

"Is she okay?"

"We don't want that to happen again. She's to go on total bed rest, no movement that might exacerbate the contractions. We'll keep that baby in utero as long as we can."

I take over as Mom and Dad, transportation chairman, chief cook and homemaker. Every second counts. As each hour passes, we say a little prayer of gratitude. Each day is a victory. When two weeks pass, we begin to relax. If born now, the baby moves from "might be viable" to "a good chance of survival." After four weeks, we're into safe territory, experienced, confident we can handle anything. Three weeks before her due date, Dr. Granton tells us, "Wendy can get up now. The danger is passed. It was Braxton-Hicks contractions, false labor. No problem."

As it turns out, Caitlin is almost a week overdue when born. But the moment she enters the world, the doctor grabs her, cuts the cord, and disappears, calling out "Blue baby! Blue baby!"

I have no idea what a blue baby is, but I know they have taken our baby away in an urgent, unexpected maneuver. A few minutes later, they return. "Here she is. You have a healthy baby girl, seven pounds, two ounces." A blue baby just needs some extra oxygen.

And so we are five. Caitlin is bathed in bliss when the nurse comes to the house two days after her birth for a well-baby check. I hold her hand, tiny fingers like new buds on the pine tree, her soft palm like the fuzz of a new peach, the smile of peace and acceptance, wavy eyelashes, total trust in the hands that hold her. I hold her as the nurse draws blood from her heel. My daughter looks up at me and howls, the sound of betrayal, the end of trust, all aimed directly at me. I am her tormenter. I tell her it is all for her own good, but she doesn't buy it. Two days old and already our relationship is in trouble. As they told me in Quadrinity, all parents mess up.

I've made great progress since Quadrinity. I exult in the joys of family and work. But all is not well. I wake each morning with a sense of foreboding. Why these dark moods that appear and disappear, uninvited, sinister? I am still hosting a terrorist movement bent on my destruction, waiting for its moment.

Chapter 28

As I climb out of the bathtub, Wendy's tone sounds like a tsunami alert. "Peter, what's wrong with your right leg?"

"My leg? It's wet. What do you——"

"It's so skinny, like a toothpick compared to the left one. Something is wrong. You need to see a doctor."

Two weeks later, my doctor shakes his head. "You've lost a lot of muscle mass. I want you to see a neurologist. Meanwhile, to be on the safe side, I'd like to do a routine physical."

I'm mildly concerned about the leg, but the physical is a non-event. A few days later, I get a return call from the receptionist. "Doctor would like you to come in for a follow-up consultation."

"Can we talk over the phone?" I ask.

"He needs to see you."

"I'm going out of town."

"He told me to schedule the visit right away."

I'm more used to having doctors tell me the first available appointment is five weeks from next Thursday. At the meeting, the doctor wastes no time. "Several of your lab reports were abnormal. Your PSA, which measures abnormalities in the prostate, was high. I want you to visit a urologist. They'll do further tests."

"Why would a urologist examine my leg?"

"It's not about the leg. You need to resolve this first."

Two weeks later, after a series of lab tests, X-rays, and a biopsy, while we're on vacation at Lake Tahoe, a call from the urologist removes any uncertainty.

"You're young for this kind of prostate cancer," he tells me. "The pathologist has confirmed an aggressive tumor. You need to deal with it."

"Deal with it?"

"I recommend surgery. Get a second opinion if you like."

"And if I don't...deal with it?"

"You'll have a few years. Barring a miracle, it will kill you."

Wendy and I talk it over, but the decision makes itself. We opt for surgery, as soon as possible.

After the surgery and a short recovery period, I am more on track than ever. The cancer feels like a speed bump, nothing more. My life is finally coming together. I have it all: a wife I love, a family I love, a career I love. Tests show no residual cancer. I own a home. I am ready to roll with the joys of life.

Not so fast.

It's nine months, almost to the day, after the surgery when the demons of doubt seize their moment to invade, descend with a vengeance, bringing suitcases and furniture, settling in to my psyche, ready apparently for a lengthy stay. *You're a fraud. You're a loser. Why should anyone like you?* Where do these voices come from? Why now?

I know their moves, this sleeper cell of terrorists, waiting for their moment. A short attack, then they withdraw. "Get out," I scream. "I banished you years ago." A few weeks later, they are back, sneaky and seductive. The attacks build in frequency and severity. "We are here," they chuckle. "And you are powerless."

One morning I wake up, covered in sweat, so filled with dread, I'm barely able to pull the covers back. My body is a cement truck. "Ten more minutes," I tell myself, but when the ten minutes is up, I need ten more and then ten more. An hour later, I am still in full retreat, in the fetal position, covers pulled over my head, "closed until further notice" the sign I'd like to display.

I force myself to go to work, but it takes me twenty minutes of sitting in the car before I can turn on the ignition. I drive ten miles an hour, down the freeway and across the Golden Gate Bridge, commuters behind me honking and giving me the finger. I arrive and park the car but lack the will to open the door. I sit in the parking lot, in total paralysis. When I am sure there is no one near, I drag myself out, slouch against the car. I am weak. Why am I weak? I must be strong. I stumble into the office, sneak around, hoping no one will see me. An hour after I sit at my desk, I take out a pencil. An hour later, I put it back in the drawer. I drag through the day. Even the decision to get a cup of coffee is filled with fear and doubt. I am the shadow of a shadow, a deflated balloon, filled with shame and doubt.

Driving home from work, I am drowning in the overwhelming sadness of being. Crossing the Golden Gate Bridge —the timing is classic—I watch a man in a lemon-yellow sweatshirt and jeans steal one last glance at passing traffic before the final, fateful leap, two hundred feet down to icy freedom. Traffic slows, a cacophony of horns and slamming brakes, drivers themselves eager to escape, desperate for something, anything, what? Who knows? Even the euca-lyptus leaves on the headlands are weeping. I should drive on forever, to the end of this earth, out of this shit life, like the yellow sweatshirt, at least he's taken action, over the cliff, into the eternal blackness that, sooner or later, is my destiny, so why not get on with it?

I make it home, then collapse on the couch. Wendy is eternally patient. I am eternally boring. A week later, I'm pinned in bed until noon, then able only to shuffle from room to room, looking for a place in the house that is not infested by the demons. No such spot exists. The windows laugh at me. The doors slam in my face. Cobwebs of misery trap me wherever I go. I can't eat. I can't sleep.

Wendy is the essence of love and caring. She has retrained and is now a licensed therapist. "I'm a total disaster, but there's nothing wrong with me," I drone on like a broken record.

Wendy knows desperation when she sees it. "You're not yourself."

"Then who am I?"

"You have to see a doctor," she says.

All day, I stare out the window, sealed in a catatonic bubble. Doug and Gavin have both left the home, off to college and life. Caitlin skirts around me as she passes on her way to and from school. She doesn't know what to think of me. I don't know what to think of me either.

Then suddenly, magically, the cloud lifts, as effort-lessly as the sun rises in the morning and sweeps aside the darkness. I am exultant. I have a life again. "See," I tell Wendy. "Whatever it was, it's gone."

"I'm so glad," she says. Her eyes hold a deeper truth.

I am back at work and back at play. I put the dread times behind me. Good to go.

None is so foolish as the fool who fools himself. Like a marauding enemy who withdraws briefly to regroup, the demons return. I know what to expect. I am a depression recidivist, returning to prison for a life sentence. I know the terror of long nights in cold cells. I bargain with God. "Get me out of here. I'll do anything. I'll donate everything I have to the poor, become a missionary in Africa, live on bread and water, just free me from this dread." God is on vacation.

It's worst in the morning. A whole day until I can go to sleep again. I try to eat but gag on anything. I'm reduced to Ensure, the kind of drink I associate with the old and the demented. Is that me? I would trade depression for dementia. At least I wouldn't be conscious. I struggle to keep my condition a secret, but I am sure everyone knows, everyone is talking. Despair is the background of every moment of every day, except when it's the foreground.

I drag myself to work. *Do they know? Of course, they know. Everyone knows. They're all talking about me. What do they think? Are they laughing at me? They are scoffing, deriding me for my weakness.*

One morning, I slink off to the men's room at nine thirty and spend the rest of the day there. Every hour or so there's a knock on the door, then the shuffle of feet. My partners, I'm sure, are trying to figure out how to get rid of me. I will soon be fired, and when I lose my job, I will lose my house, and when I lose my house, my family will leave me, and without family or house or job, I will wander the streets babbling incoherently, lugging around my black plastic garbage bag of dirty clothes on my back, and I will cease to eat or wash until I am so weak and weary and so repulsive that no one will approach me, and then I will collapse in the gutter and die alone and unnoticed and that will be best for all.

Perhaps the Catholics have it right, except they think Hell is in the afterlife. Hell, I conclude, is now, second after second, minute after minute, hour after hour, day after day, and night after night. There is no end, except in death.

Wendy is the only person I can talk with. "I can't go on."

"That's not you speaking."

"No? Then who?"

"It's the disease. It's the depression."

Unable to work, I take a leave of absence. My partners are totally understanding. *I don't deserve such understanding. I haven't even earned the right to be depressed. I've led a privileged life. I have no excuse. Except my own weakness.*

I am tired beyond hope. I repeat the same words, the same hopeless images. Wendy listens, but she can't understand. No one could understand. "I'm weak. I should be able to overcome this. Why do I have such pathetic willpower?"

"It's the chemistry in your brain," Wendy insists. "You're not weak. You're sick. You can't help it."

The more I fight, the worse I get. The worse I get, the more ashamed I feel. The more ashamed I feel, the closer to signing out forever. I am slipping down an insidious spiral, into the blackest, deepest pit where the most wretched of the wretched swim in squalor. *And I will never get out.*

Nothing consoles me. Dealing with cancer was so much easier than this. Cancer was an external threat, yes a lethal struggle, but something concrete and definable, something to problem solve, clear battle lines drawn, and an action plan. This is different. The enemy is me. There is no obvious path of action, no guarantee of anything except the relentless, debilitating drumbeat of hopelessness.

Wendy sets me up with a psychiatrist. The psychiatrist sets me up with antidepressants. I take them as prescribed, but with no faith and no enthusiasm. "I hate the pills," I tell him.

"You want to get better." Dr. Akers leans back in his chair. "You'd take aspirin if you had a fever. Think of the pills like aspirin for the brain."

I visit Dr. Akers regularly. "Do you ever consider harming yourself? Do you feel worse in the morning or the evening? On a scale of one to ten?"

"Ten," I snap at him.

"You've been depressed on and off for years. It's like any disease that goes untreated." I dislike his smug diagnosis and his unctuous probing. The days are interminable. The sleepless nights, still longer. I don't deserve Wendy's love and attention. She gives me simple assignments to keep me busy: weed the driveway, cut the blackberry bushes, routine tasks prescribed to keep my mind occupied. I pull at the weeds, arms and legs slow and heavy, like swimming through molasses.

Wendy is at work. Caity is at school. I've existed but barely, outside in the blackberry patch for a couple of hours, pretending to trim. I enter the house through the attached garage, roam about in the kitchen, searching for something, I've no idea what, but it's the pills that step forward, off the counter and into my hand. Some force rises up inside and takes over, like a mythological beast, no questions, no permissions granted. I hurl the vial of pills across the room and watch them spill out, small and white, against the red Mexican-tile floor. I want to crush the little buggers into oblivion. They laugh at me. I kick at them, hit one or two, but mostly they escape my wrath. I hate the pills. I don't know why.

I'm breathing harder as I head up to the garage. I've been thinking about it for some time, but I've never said the words, not even to myself. Somewhere on the stairs, maybe about the fourth or fifth stair up, I make the decision, or rather the decision makes me. I slow my pace, feel a sense of calm for the first time. I don't need to bother about the pills or Dr. Akers or the shame or the gloom. Never again. The garage wall is rimmed with rough shelves I built some time ago. I survey the shelf contents and wonder what they will do with all the stuff after I'm gone? I stare at the rafters for a few minutes, then fetch a small climbing stool, and climb up. Standing on top of the stool, I can easily reach the rafters. I lift my legs off the stool, test to be sure the rafters will support my weight.

Of course. It will be over soon.

I shut the garage door. I need about six feet of rope. I scrounge through the shelves. There's twine, but it's not strong enough. I toss over boxes, tear into drawers, chuck the contents aside, more desperate now, feeling the urgency. Is this God's bad last joke? Broken cups, old tools, empty paint cans, towels, and T-shirts soon litter the floor. I'll go to the hardware store. *Now where are the car keys? How hopeless am I? I can't even find the car keys.* I go back inside the house. Chest of drawers, on the counter, kitchen cabinets, hall table, under the bed. *Where? I am finally free of the doubt, free to do what I should have done years ago, clear, certain, on the track, and now I can't find the bloody car keys. I have an hour before Wendy will be home. Maybe the keys are in the car, under the mat. Yes, she might have left them there.*

Back to the garage, I hunt through the same shelves I've already searched. Is this to be my last, final indignity, unable to find the car keys, a two-inch nothing blocking my will, an inanimate piece of metal thwarting me, laughing at me. Is this my true fate?

Under the car seat. Yes, that's where I was going to look.

I open the car door, bend over the seat and reach under, feel across the carpet until my fingers touch something. I wrap my fingers around them, unmistakable. A sense of peace settles over me as I pull them out, then slide into the driver's seat. *It won't be long now. Ten minutes to the hardware store. It'll all be over in half an hour.*

I start the car. Just as I reach for the garage door opener, I hear the strain of an engine coming up the driveway. Quickly I press the remote again to close the door. *I have to cover up.* I'm out of the car, trying to kick some of the mess I'd made into the corner. The garage door swings open. Wendy greets me. She doesn't seem to notice the mess.

"Hi. I came home early. I was so worried about you. How are you?"

It's a real question. I survey the garage, hoping she won't notice. "Fine."

"I see you did some weeding on the driveway."

"Mmm."

"How's the day been?"

"Lovely."

"No, seriously."

"Not so lovely." I feel her love, misplaced but genuine. Suddenly I'm glad not to be hanging from a rafter. I wouldn't want her to open the garage door and find that.

We head down to the family room, where I collapse into a chair. I don't tell her what I was doing, but she eyes me. I can't hide. I make it through the next two days. The garage is not the right approach, but I stop as I walk through the kitchen, drawn to the black-handled sharp knives. I debate which one I might use. *Where? Here in the kitchen? Too messy. The bathtub is traditional. Slit the wrists, right? Or could I take pills? How many would it require? How can I know for sure?*

I flail around in the cold and deep, thrown about by a riptide, overcome by forces darker and more frightening than anything I've known. I flail about in the terror of disorientation, panic, fear, suffocation, and the gasping for air that is not to be had. I am drowning. The more I struggle, the deeper I sink, there to languish forever as the clock ticks and tocks its way across the hours, days that ooze into weeks, snail time, weeks that topple into months. Yes, there is a Hell, and I am in it.

✱

Wendy accompanies me on my weekly appointment with Dr. Akers. He probes. I tell him about my suicidal fantasies. He leans forward. "Can you guarantee me that you won't hurt yourself?"

In my mind, I see the kitchen drawer opening, the knives seem to rise up out of the drawer. "No."

"I can check you into the hospital."

"I don't want to go to the hospital."

"Just for a while. You want to get better. They'll help you get beyond this crisis period."

I have no counterargument. No resistance left in me. I pack my bag: toothbrush, razor, shampoo, a pencil, hair brush, pajamas, shirts, and pants. Wendy drives me to the hospital, poking at conversation. "I told them we'd be there by four, but I don't think we will."

"Mmm."

"It'll be good for you."

On a narrow street near the hospital, cars speed by, a couple talks casually on the sidewalk, a dog sniffs the curb, normal, part of a twilight zone, not my world. We pull into the hospital parking lot. Wendy looks at me. A wan smile. I work to summon a response, but my smile muscles have died. She leads the way, up the concrete stairs, footsteps that echo across the bookends of my life, through the metal swing gate, through the double doors, above the squeak of our shoes, under the fluorescent lights, past the prints of contented, grazing deer; through the lingering smell of antiseptic cleanliness, until we reach the sign: "Psychiatric Unit—Floor 3."

The door thuds behind us. My new home.

Chapter 29

I slouch over the reception desk and eye the time cards lined up on the wall. The workers here sign in and sign out. I am signing in. I don't think I will be signing out any time soon.

Riley, the on-duty nurse, opens a file drawer and removes a white plastic bag. She is heavyset, with big breasts and thinning hair, dark roots pushing up into a mass of blond.

"Okay, Charles, I need to go through your things."

"It's Peter. Charles is my first name. I go by Peter."

Riley shrugs. "Your bag, please." She taps on the desk. I place my small suitcase on the spot where she tapped.

"Open it."

I follow Riley's red painted fingernails as they rummage through my bag, or is it my soul? She removes my wallet, toothbrush, razor, my shampoo, my pencil, even my hairbrush. I glance over at the wall, try to make out "The patients' Bill of Rights" posted next to the time cards, but the print is too small. "We'll keep your things here to be returned to you when you're discharged."

"Why do you want the shampoo?"

"It's the bottle."

"The bottle?" I let it go. What was I expecting? A

massage? Roses at my bedside? She puts my confiscated items in the plastic bag, labels it, and stuffs it in a locked cabinet. I reach for Wendy's hand, but she's gone. Then I remember the nurse dismissing her: "Come back for visiting hours, four to five thirty. The tech down the hall will let you out." I am alone. I hold the imprint of Wendy's arms around me. Now this.

Riley comes around the desk, takes me by the elbow, steers me—as if I can't walk—down a corridor, hospital blue-gray walls on both sides, and a faint, chemical smell. A steady thump-thump drums out of a nearby room. I spot a young man standing, back to the door, banging his fist against the wall. Riley stops to page someone: "Check on thirteen." We go through a large common area. Patients shuffle around in slippers, baggy sweaters, and sweatpants, two or three droolers, glazed-over, vacant eyes. I don't belong here. I am not one of these.

The ward is small, two hallways off one common room, one central desk area, white coats watching everything, scribbling notes, scurrying about, jangling keys, dispensing meds.

Riley opens the door to room 4-C. "This is your room."

Four blank, white walls, one metal twin bed, a dresser with three drawers, one overhead light. One small window. I try to open the window. Locked.

"Dinner will be in twenty minutes," Riley says as she closes the door. I tour my new cell, run my hand up the wall, try the tap for the sink. It works. I acknowledge the stranger in the mirror and quickly turn away. I should have brought a picture. Wife, children. A friendly face would help. I test the bed. How many crazies have slept in this bed? Did they all feel as ashamed and lost as I do? The sheets are starched and thin and smell like Tide.

I lie down on the bed and close my eyes, fold my hands across my chest. *So it's come to this.* I lie still, try not to think, not to feel, not to move. I'd be happy not to be. After a few minutes, there's a knock. "Dinner."

The common room serves as the dining room. Twenty bodies scattered about, tables of one and two and an occasional threesome. One man, at a table by himself, chatters away, gesticulating sternly about some matter of national importance, but most are silent. Riley reads out the menu. "We have a new resident," she announces, "Charles Gibb. Charles, would you like to say hello to the other residents?"

"My name is Peter," I say, but everyone is busy with their food.

So we are "residents." That, I guess, is supposed to make us feel special. Like we are hotel guests. I don't feel special. I push the food around my plate. A server comes over and tells me I should try to eat something. "That's the law?" I ask.

She scowls. They can't make me eat. I watch the forks and spoons travel from table to plate to mouth and back. Like a slow-motion movie. These people—them, us, me—it's like we are the oddball cast in a Fellini film. One woman, about thirty-five, has long, dark eyelashes that loop like a piglet's tail, and blue toenails with white polka dots. I nickname her "Eyelashes." Another woman is disguised as a bowling ball, black pants and a sleeveless black T-shirt, round rolls of flesh everywhere, and short cropped black hair. We are real; we are surreal. The orderly removes my plate. Bowling Ball turns on the TV. I slink back to 4-C.

About ten, I go to bed, climb between my starched sheets and rumble about. My mind is a thunderstorm. I'm in prison. I sweat all over, toss off the blanket, lie awake, conjuring up plans to escape. Every hour on the hour, a head pokes through the door to verify that I'm still alive. "Still here," I call out. "Unfortunately."

"Go to sleep," the attendant says.

"Go to Hell," I mumble, politely.

In the morning, we gather for group therapy. We're in the same room where we ate, but now seated in a circle of maroon plastic chairs. Everything is plastic: the chairs, the table, the floor, the people. About ten of us in a circle, plus a white coat, "B," she calls herself. Or maybe it's "Bee." Or "Be." I don't know which it is. I'll call her "B." She's a short, mousy woman with owl-like glasses, hair the color of a wilted fig. The room has windows, locked of course, overlooking an outside deck. B moves about in tiny steps, rearranging each chair an inch this way or that. One wall of the room is lined with cabinets and drawers. Two cabinet doors are open. Papers and records and boxes of I-don't-know-what. I claim a chair as close to the window as possible, then turn to gaze outside.

We go around the circle. Each person reports on how they're doing. Eyelashes's name is Isadora. She says she's a model. In her dreams. Bowling Ball calls herself Moon. One of those hippie names. Names that seek some new, supernatural identity, pretend we are not what we are. I ignore most of what is said, busy myself playing Fellini, directing a movie in my mind about patients in a mental hospital. I don't want to think about why I am here. I zoom the camera in on one of the patients, a young man about twenty. He says his name is Rabbit. I wonder what his real name is. Joe or John. Whoever heard of a name like Rabbit? Rabbit reminds me of Popeye the Sailor Man. I watch him. I'm making an art film, very avant-garde. The chair is hard. A pain shoots up my leg. Sciatica. I am fifty-two. I look like I'm 152. I feel a small dribble down my leg. I cross my legs, hoping B won't notice and demote me to the dribblers group.

"Peter, how about you? You've just joined the group. Tell us about yourself. How is it going?"

B is talking to me. I zoom in on her through my camera lens. She has a small mole just below her lips, on the left side. She uncrosses her legs, waiting for me to respond. "How is it going?" That would take a long time to answer. My camera scans the circle. "I'm here." I stare out the window. Down on the street, a woman walks a large black Lab, who stops and sniffs. I would like to be that dog.

"Anything more you'd like to share?" B asks.

"I'd like to go outside."

B considers. "You don't want to be here?"

"Everyone wants to get out of here," I say.

B raises an eyebrow. "How about you speak for yourself? Unless you've asked everyone about that."

I roll my eyes.

"You think these doors are preventing you from being free?" B continues. "Anything else that might be restricting your freedom?"

"Yeah, there is."

"And that would be?"

"You." It's not like me to talk so boldly, but here, I've nothing left to lose.

B doesn't miss a beat. "You think I'm holding you back."

I give her the duh look. She shakes her head. "There's just one person who can get you out of here. You're the one with the keys." Perhaps she hasn't noticed the ring of keys jangling at her side. "I'm here to help, but you have to do the work."

I stare at my hands. No keys there. My mind swirls around keys. How did I get in here? Of course, the garage, the rope. Dr. Akers. How do I get out?

B tires of me and moves on. I tune in, tune out. After a while, she tucks her papers into a folder. "People, we're done for today. If you'd help stack your chairs against the wall, please," I feel like I'm flying in space somewhere, nothing but space as far as I can see. Am I an airplane with just one wing, spinning around in circles? Is that who I am? Or am I an airplane that flies fine, but the pilot got lost? Am I the pilot of my own life? Or is some other force controlling me. Brain chemicals. Some people say it's all chemical. Or Professor Temple's rats. They're still with me. Or is it my mother? Is she still pulling the strings? Where am I in all of this? Do I even exist? Or am I a figment of my own imagination? A joke. Frankenstein invents Frankenstein, and believes his own story.

Isadora combs her hair in her pocket mirror. She glances furtively at me. Our eyes meet. She gives me a half-wink. I look away. How far back did it all start? This emptiness, this doubt thing, this voice that roams like a devil inside me, that I try to hide from the world. How can you hide a devil? When did it start? The race at Campusdoon School in Scotland? Or even before then? They say those things . . . I don't know. I need to know. They call it depression? Was it fate? "In the genes," as they say. Or could I have done it differently? Did I bring this internal civil war on myself? Or was it an accumulation of psychic slaps and bruises? I was drawn into the darkness. I sought it out, why? As a lonely teen, I sat in my room playing one sad song after another. I couldn't get enough sadness. I chose sadness. How sick is that?

Time on the ward staggers forward, each day more dead than its predecessor. How long have I been here? Does it matter? Hour after hour, an endless shuffling of bodies and souls, meds parceled out in small paper cups, murmured voices of quiet resignation. Fear and failure. Group in the morning. Group in the afternoon. I've grown accustomed to Isadora, the model, and Moon, who I first thought of as a bowling ball, and Rabbit, the muscleman, who looks like Popeye the Sailor—the same lock of dark hair that Popeye had, falling across his forehead. Like Popeye, Rabbit wears a white T-shirt, sleeves rolled high to show off his biceps. B favors pantsuits, pink today, an oval grease spot on the left sleeve, just above the elbow. To pass the time in group, I follow the lines on the linoleum floor, a three-dimensional blue and gray cube pattern, a meandering tunnel to the other side of nothing, lines leading to lines, boxes within boxes.

"You, Peter?" B says. "You were quiet in group this morning. How are you?"

I shrug my shoulders. B is impatient with me. I don't blame her. I don't pay attention, preferring to work on my imaginary movie, trying to find the best angle to film Rabbit in his muscleman tee shirt. I don't relate to these people. I don't relate to anyone. Rabbit flexes his biceps. I watch.

Knowing you're at the bottom is strangely liberating. My pride is gone, my soft underbelly exposed. I have nothing left to defend. I laugh out loud.

"What are you laughing at?" B asks.

I look away.

"What does the silence mean?" she asks.

B's questions annoy me. I shake my head. Normally I would feel obligated to say something. Now I have nothing to say. *The silence. It just is. It's me.*

I focus my imaginary camera on Rabbit, settle back to watch. I breathe deeply, in, out, in, out. It feels good, focus only on the breath. Take it in. My attention, pulled. Where? Why? My breath. No, but a scent, a particular smell, familiar, but…and then I catch it, the lingering chemical smell of the cleaning solution they use on the floors. I bend over, so I can actually get closer to the smell. Where have I smelled that same scent before? Institutional. But where? Distant. And now I'm tumbling across time and space. Like a movie on rewind, I'm speeding back, across the years. *Back to my college days, back to that horrible apartment, the mole house, but I'm not in the apartment, no, a bigger building, but a narrow hallway and I am there, of course, yes, Chapin House, the mental hospital where I volunteered freshman year in college, yes, that's it, the same smell, the same cleanser they used there, and that nurse, what was her name, the one who, so arrogant she was. Do mental hospitals still use the same cleanser? Mildred, that was it. Does the chemical purify the demons too? I am walking down the corridors now, looking in rooms to see…a big guy, a lock of dark hair tumbling across his forehead. We make eye contact. He smiles at me. I smile back, the first time I've smiled in weeks. A rush of warmth, a burst of sunshine. This big guy. His name? I reach back into time. He looks just like Popeye. And then it's there. Charlie! Of course, Charlie, Charlie. The one who hadn't spoken in a year, who broke his silence to talk with me, so long ago. I see his face clearly now, and I see why I've been watching Rabbit.*

Rabbit looks so much like Charlie. Like Popeye. I remember how open I felt when I was with Charlie. How easy to accept him, be there, be open to the moment. Now I am the patient. Now I am closed and fearful and critical and silent. The way Charlie was. I remember Mildred telling me how sick Charlie was and how I should stay away from him and how I ignored her advice because I wanted to be there for Charlie and I knew I had something to give him, even if I wasn't sure what it was. So I opened my heart to him and I listened. I tried to be kind. That's all. And somehow it was enough.

The sun floods through the window. I am back in group, the soft shadow of the pine trees spreading across the linoleum floor. Easier now, less tense. It's good to think about Charlie again after so many years. I glance across the room at Rabbit. *So much like Charlie, though many years younger is Rabbit, is Charlie, is, who is, or is my mind playing tricks on me again or is Charlie here but don't be silly because things like that don't really happen or do they and am I more crazy than ever as Charlie settles in next to me and I smile I actually smile with my thoughts bouncing across decades, my heart speeding up and a new sense of excitement and an old friend.* "Charlie, you came all this way, across all these years, to visit me?"

Charlie's turn to smile. His hand on my arm. I reach out to touch him, not there but real. As real as the doubt that has dominated my life. As real as the stories I've been telling myself. I hear a voice. He's saying something but his lips don't move.

"Charlie, what are you saying?"

"Peter. What is it?" Now it's B's voice. I hear her voice but she's from another world, too far away to hear. It is Charlie I want to speak with. Charlie is here.

Charlie's voice sounds more like music. A warm breeze wafts across, and I'm back on the Brown campus again. Springtime. I feel the sun on my neck. The smell of the grass. Soft grass. I'm resting my hand on the grass. Sandals off. Grass against bare feet. Charlie sitting next to me, chewing a blade of grass. A bell rings in the background. Students walk by: a couple, arms around each other; a boy strolling down the brick path, lost in a book. I am eighteen years old again, the world a stage, spread out in front of me. Waiting for the play to start. What I see depends on where I look. Some areas are dark. Some are light. I will write the play. I will tell the story.

I hear voices. I lean toward Charlie. He nods. He speaks, or is it a breeze? "Let it be." He smiles at me. "Open your heart, pay attention, let it be."

"Let what be? What do you mean?"

He looks into my soul, a look I'll never forget. "Pay attention. Let it be."

"Charlie!" I want to touch him, to see if he's real, or . . . Can I trust? Or do I doubt? He is the brother I never had. I haven't seen him in decades, but we've been through a war together. We've survived, made it somehow. I want to wrap my arms around him. I'd never noticed before, but he looks a bit like me, like he might be my own reflection, or he is me, or am I going crazy, or sane, and then he's gone, and I am left to wonder. Is he real? Or is he just my imagination? And is the imagination not real, anyway? Am I back in college or am I…where am I? Who am I?

"Peter, have you done anything today that you feel good about?"

It's B of course. Her questions. The hospital. Group. The depression. But the words, Charlie's words. The doubt. "Let it be." Isn't that what he said? Was he talking about the doubt? Let it be. But I want to get rid of it. What is he saying?

I'm sitting on my maroon plastic chair, across from Rabbit, and next to Moon. I am stunned. If I were religious, I'd say I've had a visit from God. But I'm no longer religious and it wasn't God, unless God is code for whatever is beyond my ability to comprehend. Not God, but Charlie. Unless God is Charlie. Charlie is God. Words. Useless words. Let it be. I blink, back into the old reality. But it's different. "Open your heart. Pay attention," that's what Charlie said. I look about. Isadora's eyelashes, which I had thought were so affected, don't seem so affected. In fact, they are soft and pleasing. Moon's smile is so much more vital than her shape. B is silent. I hear Charlie's voice again, echoing across time: "Let it be. Let it be." The rhythm. Repetition. Easy to sing. Words wash over me. "Open your heart. Pay attention. Let it be."

One moment it's clear and reassuring, the next moment, the Earth rumbles and my brain tumbles. I close my eyes again. I feel a surge of energy, then I'm lost again. Charlie's hand rests on my arm, a slight pressure. Warm. Comforting. But is this real, or is this some new, demonic gesture to throw me off? A flash of recognition. The moment. If I seize it. If I dare. I can do it. Do what? That voice again. Charlie's voice? My voice? Pay attention to what? When it happens, it's so quick, I barely notice. Like a quick change in weather. I sense the shift. Like I've changed clothes. More than clothes, I've changed skin. Not so much a choice, but an acceptance.

I surrender. That simple. And that complicated. I am spinning, but in a new world. I know something I didn't know before. I don't need to lug this stuff around anymore. Like Charlie said, "Let it be." The whole story, the fraud thing, the loser. It's a story. I made it up. I can let it go. I made up the suffering. Let it be.

"I will."

Was that me? Did I say "I will"? Or was that Charlie? Is Charlie a figment of my imagination? A part of me? Or maybe it would have happened without Charlie. "I will" sounds like a decision. But is it a decision? It feels more like an unfolding. Suddenly it is. What is "it"? Is "it" real or just imagined? Who's to say? Who cares? I open my eyes. The room is unchanged: the maroon plastic chairs, the half-open cabinets, the windows out to the street, B's pink pantsuit, the same grease spot still above the elbow. I look at each detail, at everything around me. "Pay attention." B is leaning forward now, talking intently to Moon. Rabbit stares at the linoleum floor, the same blue and gray linoleum floor that was always there, but different.

Something has changed. No Big Bang, barely a squeak. Quiet. Intimate. No one else notices. Not that the Doubt is totally gone, but it is leaving. The unnecessaries falling away. The desire to please. The fear of being discovered.

Stories, they're just stories I made up. There and then, in group, in front of B and Isadora and Moon and Rabbit, I open my heart. I notice. I let it be. I stop fighting the doubt and the shame and let them be there, let them sit there with me while B is still talking to Moon and Rabbit is still staring at the floor and I stare at the floor and suddenly I realize: Nothing has changed and everything is different.

I take a few deep breaths. I look out the window, take it all in. I smile. Not that the doubt has gone, but it is less menacing. I am not wrapped in shame. The doubt sits there like some other patient in the hospital. I notice the doubt, but I am not the doubt. In that moment, I know that I will soon feel the sun on my back again. I am not going to die in the gutter.

That afternoon, I participate, openly and genuinely, for the first time, in group. It's fun. I assist around the ward setting up and taking down chairs and tables. I feel like I've taken a warm shower and washed away years and inches of crud that wasn't me but that I'd carried around for so long it had become me. Shame gives way to a calm and quiet pride. I listen to other patients, and to myself. I am not a bad person. I lost my way, that's all. When I was little, I wanted to be a superstar. I wanted to be the one to do the victory lap at Wimbledon, holding the big silver cup above my head, the crowd cheering. I see now that no matter how hard I work, how many mountains I climb, I will never hold that cup. And nor do I need to. I have been grasping at a dream of success defined by everyone but myself. My light is bright enough.

It takes time to integrate what Charlie said. I don't really understand it, but I trust it. Faith over doubt. I practice on the ward, opening my heart, even to B. I smile at her, wanting to see if she will smile back. What I notice is that I feel free in a way I haven't for years. I am sitting in the big room gazing out the window, thinking about what Charlie said, when my doctor stops by, asks how I'm doing. I tell him that I am ready to leave the hospital. He slips off his glasses, twirls them for a moment. "So soon. What has changed?"

"Everything."

"Everything?" He takes out a pencil and writes something in his notebook. "You're taking your meds regularly. Seems like they're helping."

"I'm ready."

He writes something more. "Depression is slippery. It goes deep. You think you've got a handle on it, then it comes back around, from a new direction."

"I am ready to go."

He shakes his head. "I can't in good conscience agree with that. I'll note your wish. You committed yourself voluntarily. I'll observe you over the coming days and confer with your psychiatrist."

"Do that," I say, and smile. He's watching me. "I'll wait a few days, so you can catch up."

He nods, then walks away.

Room 4-C embraces me after dinner. So much has happened. I close the door behind me, stretch out on the bed. I wonder where B is and what she is doing. My thoughts shift to Wendy, Caity, Doug, and Gavin. *My family. The people I love.* I feel my heart expanding. I hold my family close to me and feel the warmth of our love for one another and how I am finally ready to open my heart and let it be. I can embrace the love or I can embrace the fear. My choice. I am not Professor Temple's rat. And even if I am part rat, I can opt out of the rat race.

If I am not the king of doubt that I've been for so many years, then who am I? For a moment, I feel myself diving into worry about that one. But I catch myself. I notice. I laugh. Out loud, I laugh. Let it go. Let that question go. It's a good question - for some other day.

A warmth spreads throughout my body, in my chest, my shoulders, neck, everywhere. I scan my struggles over the decades, and I see clearly, maybe for the first time, the hopelessness and the wonder of my life. I am waking up. I thought the enemy was out there. I blamed my parents, my fears, my job, my teachers, my bank account, my cancer. But these are bumps on the twisted path, teachers if I choose to listen, stories I told myself for too long, stories that kept me locked in a limited world, stories I no longer need to tell.

I hear a knock on the door. "Yes." But no one enters. I turn towards the door. Charlie is standing there. "Charlie!" I leap out of bed. The door is closed. I open it. No one. I look up and down the hall. Quiet, dark. "Charlie." I whisper his name, expecting.

"What are you doing?" It's the night orderly.

"I'm…" He waits, but I can't finish the sentence.

"Go back to bed." He ushers me back into my room, helps me into bed, then closes the door. I lie there, thinking about Charlie. How to explain what has happened? It doesn't fit with anything that I ever learned in school. Or church. Or on the tennis court. And yet. Charlie was here. Charlie and I are connected, beyond what I thought was real or possible. I didn't understand it when I was there for him decades and thousands of miles ago. Nor do I understand how he came here for me when I most desperately needed him. What I know is that we are one, part of something beyond him, beyond me, beyond doubt, beyond understanding.

And then, I drift off to sleep, exhausted, loved, and awed by the wonder of it all.

✱

A few days later, the doctor approaches me in the hallway. "I've been watching you. I've prepared the papers for your discharge."

I smile. It's a new day.

"There is one last, essential part of the deal," he says.

He pushes his glasses up his nose. They slip back down. He looks over them, at me. I wait, wondering what he has in mind. "You *must* keep taking your meds." He pauses. "You feel good now, but you can relapse any time. The meds are what does it, they maintain your brain chemistry at a more constant level."

"Like a rat," I say.

"Huh?"

"How long?" I ask. "A month? Six months?"

"Forever."

Wendy picks me up from the hospital. Being home with her and Caity feels natural and right. The hospital episode fades into the background. Was that really me? Wendy is ever vigilant. "I know you don't like the meds," she says. "But promise me you'll take them. You don't want a relapse."

"Gotta go," I say. "Got a meeting in forty-five minutes."

"Promise?"

I nod. I'm out the door.

Within a few months, despite Dr. Akers's insistence, identical to the hospital psychiatrist, that I must stay on antidepressants for the rest of my life, I flush my supply of pills down the toilet, watch them spin about and disappear. I don't tell Wendy. One day, when I'm not even thinking about it, the news leaks out. She gasps. "But the doctors all said—"

"I know what the doctors said."

She stiffens. "You promised you wouldn't stop without telling me."

"I know."

"You broke your promise."

"Yes, I did."

Wendy is disappointed in me, fearful that the depression will return. The whole ordeal has taken a huge toll on her. She sees the pills as an essential part of sustaining my recovery. Most mental health professionals agree. No doubt it is true much of the time, but I have a new confidence in my own voice that tells me I don't need these pills. I am not a rat. I can choose. And my happiness, ultimately, is dependent on my choice. Pain and disappointment are part of life; misery is optional. I chose misery for too long, never realizing that I had a choice. Now I'm ready to move on. I am an old house with a new foundation, made from the few, simple words that Charlie whispered to me in the hospital: *Open your heart. Pay attention. Let it be.* I still don't understand the full meaning of these words, but I repeat them over and over. They fill me with life and hope.

Before Charlie, I would have caved in to the pressure and gone back to the pills. But I have found a new home and a new voice. I listen closely because I trust this voice, my voice.

I think back to that muddy race at Campusdoon School, in Scotland, so long ago. A hollow victory it was. I paid a heavy price. But what a journey it has been, wandering the twisted path, from doubt to wonder. That feels like victory to me.

Epilogue

Looking back, it is obvious that I suffered from chronic depression, during college and for many years after. At the time, I recognized that something was wrong, but I lacked the language to speak and I was too ashamed to tell, about the dark force that was robbing me of motivation, confidence, and hope. I thought I had let down the whole world. My only path, so I reasoned, was to keep my shame a secret. More than anything, it was the secrecy that crowned me "King of Doubt" and condemned me to darkness. The depression was the first arrow that wounded me severely. Shame was the second, a poison arrow, perhaps even more deadly than the first.

It has been two decades since the events of this book. In that time, there have been highs and lows, but nothing remotely like the gloom and guilt that I had fashioned into the story of my life. Writing *King of Doubt* catapulted me out of that old story. I realized that I had had a serious depression, but that I am much more than my depression. Through the writing, I finally became, on multiple levels, the author of my own story.

To all those who might be suffering from depression now or in the future, please understand this: as overwhelming and immutable as depression feels, it is not a life sentence. It is, in fact, one of the most treatable mental illnesses. I am not a trained psychologist, but I know a few things about depression: No matter how bleak it may seem, there is always some ray of light somewhere. Hold onto hope, like your life depends on it. Because it does. Find the joy in little things—a cup of coffee in the morning, a walk in the afternoon, the sight of a red-winged blackbird in flight. Let yourself feel even the briefest moment of joy. Start there. Let it build.

Another factor in my recovery was a matter of discovering what I call in this book my "voice." Voice need not necessarily consist of words. It may be exercise. Or nature. Spiritual or religious faith, diet or creative expression, or service to others. Cars, cooking, carpentry. Work, family, adventure of some kind. There are so many tools for expressing yourself. Avoid the usual addictive substances—drugs, alcohol, compulsive sex, compulsive eating, gambling, etc.—then find your voice and ride it to glory.

A word about pharmaceutical solutions to depression. Antidepressants are now widespread in our culture and have mitigated the suffering for millions of people. Mental health professionals attest to the efficacy of these little wonders. I used and benefitted from antidepressants. For me, the combination of medication, talk therapy, and the blessed presence of a loving, patient wife got me past the worst of it. My path dictated that I had to separate from the pills, but I am not advocating that for others. Mindfulness and creative expression became my lifelong therapists.

Charlie's message was the first hint of a mode of being that I now think of as mindfulness. Mindfulness—the dual practice of opening your heart and quieting your mind—revealed a new world for me. It gave me a foundation for inner peace and strength that I had never known. The practice of mindfulness, along with creative expression, became my platform for well-being and joy in subsequent years. My life turned from a dull gray to technicolor. From doubt to wonder.

If mindfulness is of interest to you, I encourage you to investigate this ancient, yet entirely modern, way of being. To learn more, see my website (www.petergibb.org) or browse the many great books, websites, workshops, and teachers on the subject. If you want scientific data, mindfulness has been researched and its benefits documented widely by multiple independent studies. Mindfulness is now used in hospitals and schools, in prisons and police academies, in business and in therapy, as an aid in combating physical, emotional, and spiritual trouble. The practice of mindfulness has become like an old friend to me. It is my "bridge over troubled water."

I am blessed indeed that our daughter, Caitlin, and my two stepsons, Doug and Gavin, are all engaged in pursuing positive life paths. The next generation is on its way. When Doug and Gavin started calling me "Dad," I felt as proud and loving toward them as if they were my own children. Decades after the events of this memoir, I learned that they had first asked their father, Greg, for his permission to call me dad. Greg graciously agreed. We became "co-dads." Subsequently, we (Wendy, our children and their families, including Greg's second wife, Connie, and her daughter, Rachel) became a blended family, celebrating holidays together, loving and supporting one another through our individual journeys, joys, and struggles. This shift is proof that with a commitment to openness, love and respect, if all are willing, even the most serious breaches of the heart can be bridged. We are proud, and all the richer for this wonderful transformation. But that's another story.

When I retired from Interaction Associates, Wendy and I moved to Ashland, Oregon. It was like coming home. Ashland was, in a very real sense, where I first began to wake up, thanks to the amazing workshop sponsored by Carl Rogers, who remains to this day one of my all-time heroes.

To Charlie, I say a deeply felt "thank you." I was lucky enough to be able to give him something I didn't even know I had in his time of need. He returned, so many miles and so many years later, and ministered to me in my time of need. And that's the way the world works, when it works, at its best.

Discussion Questions

1. In chapter 1, Peter writes, "The first time you tell yourself a story about yourself, it's a story. The second time you tell the same story, it becomes a theory. The third time you tell the story, it becomes The Truth." What stories does Peter tell himself? What stories have you told yourself? How have these stories impacted your life? Looking back on these stories, would you agree with the author's assessment that these stories are "real" but not "true"?

2. *King of Doubt* alternates chapters between childhood and adulthood. Why do you think Peter chose to do that? What impact does it have on you, the reader?

3. If you were to write about two or three formative experiences in your childhood, what would they be? What did you learn from them? How did they help you and/or hinder you?

4. In chapter 2, Wally's rat experiment seems to contrast two opposing views of life—one that claims we have free will and one that sees us as controlled by our

heritage and conditioning. How do these contrasting points of view play out in Peter's life? What do you believe about these opposing views? Do we really have free will, or might we be significantly controlled by early conditioning, too far beneath consciousness for us to recognize?

5. Peter suffered from a severe self-doubt. Does the story give us clues about the origin of that problem? What impact did self-doubt have on his life? Do you think his depression grew out of the doubt, or was that a separate issue? What helped Peter deal with his doubt and depression? Are there other approaches you think he could or should have tried?

6. We all doubt ourselves at some time or another. What is your relationship to self-doubt? When does it show up in your life? Does it appear in waves, or is it triggered by certain circumstances? Do you have strategies for dealing with self-doubt, or do you think it is just something you have to put up with?

7. Has self-doubt ever prevented you from pursuing something you might otherwise have tried? Would you handle that situation any differently today?

8. What was your reaction to the reappearance of Charlie at the end of the book? How do you explain Charlie's appearance? What impact do you think it had on Peter? Have you ever had an experience at all similar to this?

9. One of Peter's main conclusions is that "Pain and disappointment are part of life; misery is optional. I chose misery for too long, never realizing that I had a choice." What is the difference between pain and misery? Do you agree that misery is optional? Have you ever chosen misery? Why might someone choose misery?

10. What do you think Peter meant by "the hopelessness and the wonder of life." If you could choose just two words to sum up the experience of life, what two words would you choose?

CPSIA information can be obtained
at www.ICGtesting.com
Printed in the USA
FSOW01n0656030317
31491FS